Praise for

SMOKED

★ ★ ★

"Ed Randolph and his team consistently churn out some of the most knee-buckling barbecue. I can think of no one better to capture the stories and techniques of America's most talented pitmasters."

—**STEVE FOWLER,** assistant editor for *Hudson Valley Magazine*

"Whatever Ed says I'm paying attention and taking notes."

—**GEOFF FEDER,** owner of Feder Knives

"Not only does Ed consistently produce delicious award-winning BBQ at all the shows I've been to, but laying eyes on Handsome Devils' station will stop you dead in your tracks. Somehow he manages to continuously outdo himself."

—**JOHNNY PRIME,** owner of Johnny Prime Steaks

"In all of my years on the food scene, I've noticed two things about Ed Randolph and Handsome Devil BBQ. First, they always steal the show with their amazing smoked whole animal and second, they are consistently one of the best bites at any event!"

—**MICHAEL PUMA,** founder of Gotham Burger Social Club

SMOKED

ONE MAN'S JOURNEY TO FIND INCREDIBLE RECIPES,
STANDOUT PITMASTERS AND THE STORIES BEHIND THEM

ED RANDOLPH

OWNER OF HANDSOME DEVIL BBQ

PAGE STREET
PUBLISHING CO.

PAGE STREET
PUBLISHING CO.

First published in 2019 by
Page Street Publishing Co.
27 Congress Street, Suite 105
Salem, MA 01970
www.pagestreetpublishing.com

Distributed by Macmillan, sales in Canada by The Canadian Manda Group.

23 22 21 20 19   1 2 3 4 5

ISBN-13: 978-1-62414-813-2
ISBN-10: 1-62414-813-1

Library of Congress Control Number: 2018957260

Cover and book design by Rosie Stewart for Page Street Publishing Co.
Photography by Ken Goodman

Printed and bound in the United States

TO MY GIRLS, NOELLE, LILY, EMMA AND AMAI.

AND TO MOM AND DAD.

WRITTEN IN LOVING MEMORY OF GARRY ROARK

October 2, 1951–August 27, 2018

MY BBQ ROADTRIP

★ STARS REPRESENT
CITIES VISITED

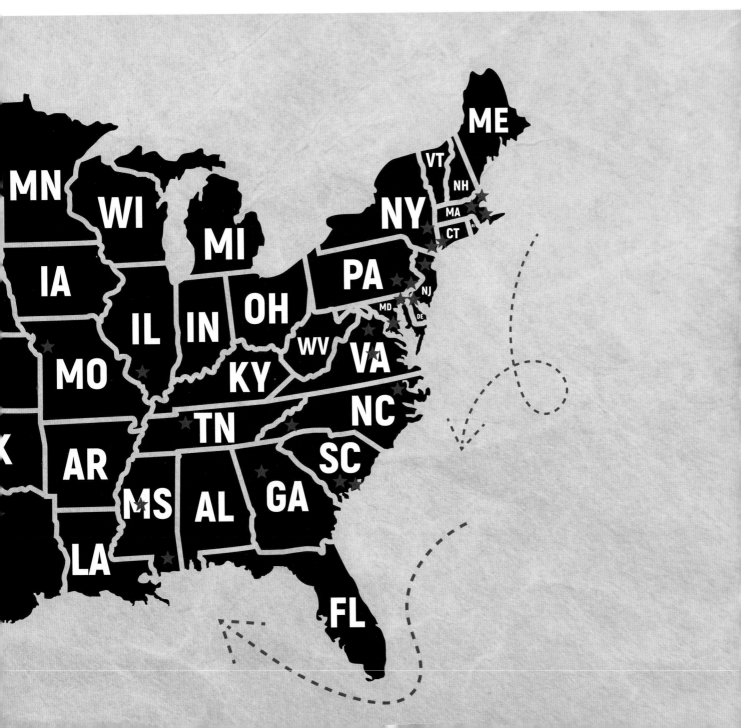

CONTENTS

FOREWORD

I've been following Ed Randolph and his Handsome Devil BBQ competition crew for the past few years. If there's anything that I've learned during that time, it's that Ed and his team are tenacious culinary warriors. They are willing to take on any challenge—no matter how crazy—and like other top national competitors, they'll do whatever it takes to make the best food and win. To date, Ed and the Handsome Devil team have won barbecue championship awards in New York, Vermont, Connecticut, Delaware and New Hampshire. They'll no doubt collect more trophies in the future.

I'm thankful to have watched Ed grow from a barbecue competitor and caterer to a true influencer and leader in the barbecue community. Ed has been part of the barbecue scene for more than twenty years. He helped make meals for Operation BBQ Relief after Hurricane Sandy devastated parts of New York and New Jersey. He frequently travels all over the country to meet with top pitmasters and take part in large events. And he's an all-around great guy and family man, even teaching his daughters how to make barbecue and shaping them into pint-size critics who can recognize what makes good barbecue.

Throughout the past few years, Ed and I have both witnessed big changes in the barbecue scene. The whole world is obsessed with barbecue these days. What started in the American South a hundred years ago is now being replicated and experimented with not only across every corner of North America but also in Asia, Australia, Europe and South America. That's a great thing for this community. If barbecue wants to truly be world-changing and be a connective tissue between cultures, it needs to fully embrace the world.

I've been based in New York City for more than ten years, and this city is emblematic of the changes barbecue is seeing globally. Here we have nearly every variation of traditional American barbecue represented, including Texas, Kansas City, North Carolina and South Carolina. But New York's chefs and pitmasters are also willing to experiment and throw out old conventions. They might smoke pork ribs or chicken wings like normal, but then they'll combine spices and flavor profiles from places like Jamaica, Korea, Vietnam and the Philippines. It's incredibly exciting.

This book features recipes and insights from pitmasters all over the country, including from places you'd expect (like Texas, Tennessee and Missouri) and from places you might not know much about (including New York, Virginia and California). This book is one part of the aforementioned global change and will show off how diverse barbecue in America has become, even including a few kosher, vegetarian and vegan recipes. Each recipe has its own ideas and brings to light the joy of barbecue in every form. I'm proud to have played a role in making this book, and I can't wait for you to read it.

—SEAN LUDWIG, founder, NYC BBQ; cofounder, The Smoke Sheet

INTRODUCTION

I could've never imagined how barbecue would change my life. The passion and patience of tending a fire has led Handsome Devil from a backyard barbecue to a Memphis in May barbecue vendor. Since my company's inception, the rules have been the same: make good traditional barbecue, empower my staff to be decision makers, never be out-hustled and create a legacy by sharing my knowledge with the next generation.

My journey into the culinary world started the same way it has for a vast majority of us—from watching my mother and grandmother cook. I was born and raised in the Hudson Valley region of New York. I come from a family with a long lineage of farming this rich area of land. There was no going out to the local marketplace or lifestyle center for dinner, because they didn't exist. Meals were made at home from scratch with love and recipes handed down from generations before.

Cooking is a passion, it is therapy and it is what makes me happy. I'd go to school to earn an economics and accounting degree, but there was always a deep burning fire for cooking. Eventually, I started to hold an annual New Year's Day barbecue party. With all of our friends and family busy during the holiday season and me suffering from cabin fever, New Year's Day was the perfect day to fire up the smoker and relax with friends. By 2011, my backyard hobby had transitioned into catering private events and to supplying barbecue to other caterers. I made the decision to launch my brand to the public.

One morning, as I prepared to begin my commute to the Big Apple, my oldest daughter, Lily, woke up at 5:00 a.m. to wish me a good day at work. From the top of the stairs she said, "Have a good day, Daddy—you're a handsome devil." My Lily just hit pure gold. By the time I reached midtown Manhattan, I had already researched the state database and soon after filed for the creation of Handsome Devil BBQ. The company was born.

My enthusiasm slowly turned to despair as I started to come to the realization that local event organizers had long-standing agreements with other barbecue vendors. No one was willing to take a chance on a new local company. I was determined to make this work, so I started to look for new events that didn't have vendors in place. I quickly figured out this meant we would have to hit the road. What I thought was a curse turned out to be a blessing. The organizers loved us and the guests enjoyed our food. We were given open invites to participate in future shows. Traveling also gave us the opportunity to experience some great barbecue in each area.

We were given an opportunity by Greg Nivens and the Trigger Agency to have a space at their annual Beer, Bourbon and BBQ Festival in frigid January in New York City. To this day, I still thank Greg for the opportunity because it put us on the map and gave us the opportunity to work alongside the legendary Bill Eason of Little Red Pig from North Carolina. We froze our butts off all night tending fires for our whole hogs. Bill had a heater and a canopy tent with sides. I was staying warm in my truck. As I was loading my firebox, he called me over to his makeshift campsite. We sat as close as we could to the heater for what felt like hours, all the time sharing stories about the good and not-so-good barbecue we have experienced on the road. Granted, Bill had many more stories than I did.

Over the next few years as we would travel, we would start to notice customers asking us if we had tried the local barbecue or for recommendations for when they traveled. I recall looking to my wife, Noelle, and saying we should write a book to feature the outstanding pitmasters we had met. Always supportive, she pushed me to pursue my dream. With the help of barbecue pitmaster and author Bill Gillespie, I was introduced to Page Street Publishing, the publishing company that would make the idea of a barbecue road trip cookbook become a reality.

Becoming a pitmaster means spending countless early mornings and late nights tending a fire. Pitmaster is not a glorious position; rather, it's sourcing a quality product, performing tedious prep, enduring long cook times and taking extensive care, all in an attempt to achieve a consistent product that people will enjoy. It is not out of the ordinary for a pitmaster to have worked fourteen hours before he or she opens the door to their first customer. Yet the popularity of barbecue is at an all-time high. There are more barbecue festivals, competitions and brick-and-mortar joints than ever before. The pitmasters in this book come for all walks of life. We met with pitmasters that have generations of barbecue in their blood; a former A-list bodyguard; a software engineer; a former real estate broker; a banquet cook; a utility company engineer; classically French-trained chefs; winners of the American Royal World Series of Barbecue®, the Jack Daniels World Championship Invitational Barbecue competitions and the Memphis in May World Championship Barbecue Cooking Contest; and James Beard nominees. The one thing all of them have in common? Their passion for barbecue. From preserving traditional recipes from generations prior to incorporating international flavors into their creations, they are all driven to share their love for everything barbecue. This book is about them.

We tried to share a variety of pitmasters with you in this book, featuring some of the most notable barbecue joints in America, award-winning competitors, top-producing concessionaires and television personalities. We made stops to more than forty pitmasters in Mississippi, Georgia, North Carolina, South Carolina, Tennessee, Massachusetts, Connecticut, New York, New Jersey, California, Maryland, Virginia, Illinois, Missouri and Texas. At each stop we tried to capture the pitmaster's story, the experience at their establishment and an authentic recipe from each. Some recipes are items on the menu, some were originally prepared for competition and some were developed for family gatherings. These are recipes directly from the pitmasters. Maybe you can't make it to Hometown Bar-B-Que in Brooklyn, New York, for an order of Korean Sticky Ribs (page 28) but you can smoke some at home and enjoy Billy Durney's passion for pushing barbecue to the next level.

Barbecue is family. It only made sense that I share this experience with my family. To most a summer family road trip to visit multiple pitmasters might sound crazy. However, it was important to me that my girls see the hard work, dedication and pride people put into their craft. Traveling from state to state, you get to see what makes America great. Drive from Atlanta to Asheville to Nashville and you will experience great barbecue, doughnuts, peaches, pecans, ice cream and caverns. Nothing can beat the hospitality of the barbecue brethren. We were welcomed with open arms at each location, treated like family and offered assistance with future legs of travel. We met up with old friends, made new ones and cultivated memories that will last a lifetime. I love barbecue, and I am grateful for the opportunities that barbecue has offered me and the people I have met along the way. I am extremely humbled to be able to share with you what makes barbecue great and where to find it. I am excited for you to read the stories of these pitmasters and share their recipes with your friends and family.

Finally, remember we all have a story we want to tell. The next time you stop at your favorite barbecue joint, take a few minutes and ask the pitmaster about their story. Every time I go to another barbecue joint and hear the pitmaster's story, I'm inspired to keep sharing mine with others. I hope you enjoy the stories of these pitmasters who have motivated me.

BUXTON HALL BAR-B-CUE

ASHEVILLE, NORTH CAROLINA   »   ELLIOTT MOSS

32 Banks Ave.
South Slope Asheville, NC
www.buxtonhall.com

Elliott Moss's barbecue DNA comes from growing up in Florence, South Carolina, where he recalls playing with pigs and chickens on his grandparents' farm. Occasionally, the family would make barbecue for the neighborhood—a whole hog on their homebuilt block pit, kettles of chicken bog and barbecue chicken were the typical menu. For Elliott, it's that tradition of honoring South Carolina barbecue that is so important to him as a head chef. Buxton Hall Barbecue is a whole-hog barbecue restaurant first and foremost. Whole hogs are cooking 24/7, and all the pork is either pulled or chopped.

In 2007, Elliott moved to Asheville, North Carolina, to help open another person's restaurant. While there, he garnered acclaim and accolades, including a James Beard nomination for best chef for his creative fare. Shortly thereafter, Moss partnered with Meherwan Irani to build his dream of an all-wood-fired, whole-hog barbecue joint. A dynamic partnership between two-time James Beard Award–nominated chef-owner Meherwan Irani and two-time James Beard Award–nominated chef Elliott Moss, Buxton Hall Barbecue was introduced to Asheville in 2015.

When I asked how Buxton Hall Barbecue got its name, Moss stated it was to pay tribute to the area. The South Slope of Asheville was historically called Buxton Hill. When they walked the space for the first time, Elliott felt like he was walking into a communal beer hall. He also learned that the space had previously served as a skating hall. Buxton Hall Barbecue was a fitting name, and it's a beautiful restaurant. An open kitchen with exposed pits entertains guests as they enjoy their food. The abundance of white subway tile, stainless steel and hardwood serves as the backdrop for the eye-catching barbecue. The food is the star here—the Buxton Hall Barbecue team makes sure it stands front and center. In 2016, Elliott released his book *Buxton Hall Barbecue's Book of Smoke*, which tells his story in detail and shares a number of his family recipes.

SMOKED WHOLE CHICKEN
WITH RED SAUCE

While Elliott is world renowned for his whole hog, his chicken dishes are equally amazing. Eight years working at Chick-fil-A paid dividends for Elliott. He has designed a crispy fried chicken sandwich with pimento cheese and white sauce that's just divine. His pit-smoked chicken and chicken bog side are just as exquisite. There is nothing like fresh-out-of-the-pit chicken. At Buxton Hall Barbecue, they coat it with a red sauce that will leave you wanting more.

COOK TIME: 2 hours   **YIELD:** 2 to 4 servings

BRINE
10½ cups (2.5 L) warm water
½ cup (120 g) salt
½ cup (96 g) sugar
½ tbsp (4 g) whole black peppercorns
½ tbsp (3 g) fennel seeds
½ tbsp (5 g) ground cumin
½ tbsp (3 g) mustard seeds

CHICKEN
1 (3-lb [1.35-kg]) whole chicken
1 batch brine
Freshly ground black pepper
3 cups (720 ml) Buxton Hall House-Made BBQ Red Sauce

To make the brine, combine the warm water, salt and sugar in a large bowl. Once the salt and sugar are dissolved, add the peppercorns, fennel seeds, cumin and mustard seeds and let the mixture steep for 20 minutes.

To make the chicken, add the chicken to the brine, cover the bowl and transfer the bowl to the fridge. Brine the chicken for a minimum of 5 hours (overnight is preferred).

Remove the chicken from the brine, pat it dry with a paper towel and sprinkle it with the black pepper.

Spatchcock or cut your chicken in half. To spatchcock, you will need a sturdy set of poultry shears. First, cut out the backbone of the chicken by cutting along both sides of the spine. Then spread the chicken's legs apart and flip it over so it's skin side up. Press down firmly on the breastbone until you hear a crack—that's the wishbone breaking, and the chicken will now lie quite flat.

Prepare a smoker to cook directly at 220°F (104°C).

Cook the chicken for 2 hours. Halfway through the cooking, dunk the chicken in the red sauce and baste it every 20 minutes thereafter. Cook the chicken to an internal temperature of 165°F (74°C).

If you prefer a crispy skin, at serving time flip the chicken over on the smoker above the hot coals to crisp it up.

CHICKEN BOG

Until I traveled to the South, I had never heard of a chicken bog. It is a recipe specific to the South Carolina region. This gumbo-like dish combines chicken and stock with sausage, rice and peas. It amazes me that this dish is relatively unheard out outside of the Carolina region.

COOK TIME: 50 minutes   **YIELD:** 10 servings (as a side)

CHICKEN BOG STOCK

1 (3-lb [1.35-kg]) whole chicken

½ cup (68 g) whole black peppercorns

½ bunch celery, coarsely chopped

1½ lb (680 g) carrots, coarsely chopped

½ bunch fresh thyme

½ tsp red pepper flakes

¼ cup (58 g) smoked hog fat or butter

9 cups (2.2 L) water

CHICKEN BOG

4 cups (840 g) uncooked long-grain rice

1 lb (450 g) smoked sausage, sliced ¼ inch (6 mm) thick

¼ cup (24 g) freshly ground black pepper

Salt, to taste

2 cups (300 g) frozen peas

To make the chicken bog stock, place the chicken, peppercorns, celery, carrots, thyme, red pepper flakes and hog fat in a large stock pot and cover the ingredients with the water. Bring the mixture to a boil over high heat. Reduce the heat to medium and simmer for 30 minutes, until the chicken is cooked through. Remove the chicken skin and set it aside. Strain the stock through a fine-mesh strainer into a large bowl. Do not skim or remove the fat. Set the stock aside.

Let the chicken cool and then pick the meat from the bones, setting the meat aside.

To make the chicken bog, transfer 8 cups (1.9 L) of the chicken bog stock to a large pot with a tightly fitting lid. Bring the chicken stock to a boil over high heat. Add the chicken, rice, sausage and black pepper. Bring the mixture back to a boil and taste for seasoning. Add salt if needed.

Reduce the heat to low and bring the mixture to a simmer. Cover the pot with the lid and cook for 20 minutes, stirring once or twice in the first 5 minutes and then leaving the lid on. Turn off the heat and let the chicken bog sit for 10 minutes. Uncover the pot, add the peas, and stir. Serve immediately.

HOMETOWN BAR-B-QUE

BROOKLYN, NEW YORK » BILLY DURNEY

454 Van Brunt St.
Brooklyn, NY 11231
www.hometownbarbque.com

The idea that great barbecue doesn't exist outside the South was debunked years ago. Not so long ago, Texas-style barbecue was impossible to find in NYC. Now, though, we've got an embarrassment of riches. However, the thought of piling into a car or mass transit and traveling to an isolated barbecue joint was, and for the most part still is, a Southern thing. That is, until Billy Durney, the undisputed king of NYC barbecue, brought his Hometown Bar-B-Que to Red Hook, Brooklyn.

Billy is a giant of a man, a great advocate for barbecue, and the only thing bigger than his heart and personality might be the giant beef ribs he makes. What Billy is doing that is so important to the world of barbecue isn't just his consistent reproductions of the Texas Trinity (brisket, sausage and pork ribs), but his ability and desire to take barbecue to a global level. His brisket, beef and pork pay homage to the mentoring he received from Mike Mills of 17th Street Barbecue (see page 76) and Wayne Mueller of Louie Mueller Barbecue of Texas. In addition, Billy is striving to find the comfort zone with various international flavors. Nowhere in New York is there more of a melting pot than in Brooklyn. When Billy opened Hometown, he wanted to share what he had learned with the local community and started to introduce new flavors. When was the last time you saw a barbecue joint with lamb belly banh mi, Jamaican jerk baby back ribs, Korean sticky ribs and Vietnamese wings on the menu?

Hometown is located on a street corner neighboring a garden center and industrial building. I could smell the smoke and see the Lang brand smokers trailer on the street before I caught a glimpse of the building. It is a large building, larger than most barbecue joints in Texas or Tennessee. Enter through the door and you will forget you are less than a handful of miles from Wall Street. It is sensory overload upon entry. The smell of smoke and instant decision making makes you stop in your tracks. Do you go to the left and get online to place your order? Or do you go to the right and belly up to an impressive bar properly fitted with a bartender wearing a flannel shirt, blue jeans and big belt buckle? I made a stop at the bar while I waited for Billy to finish talking to a customer. Billy believes barbecue's future is far greater than just pork shoulder and beef brisket and, frankly, I have no reason to disagree. He put together a sample of food for me to try while we were talking: brisket, beef ribs, Korean sticky ribs, queso mac 'n' cheese, collard greens and some tostados. You must order either the brisket or beef rib and definitely the Korean Sticky Ribs. There is a forty-five-minute wait every day at Hometown and that's fine, because Billy has made NYC barbecue a destination venue. While the phrase "a New York minute" might be true in every other borough, those traveling to Red Hook are willing to take it low and slow. With excitement, Billy shared with me that he's going to be opening a Hometown fried chicken joint and a Hometown deli in Brooklyn. With his determination and ambition, there is no doubt these, too, will be a success.

SMOKED LAMB BANH MI

When I think of barbecue, I do not initially think of lamb. However, this is another instance where Billy has incorporated the flavors and traditions of his local environment into a brilliant creation. This banh mi can rival any you would find at a local Vietnamese restaurant.

COOK TIME: 9 hours   **YIELD:** 4 sandwiches

PICKLED DAIKON AND CARROTS
2 cups (480 ml) distilled white vinegar

1 cup (240 ml) rice wine vinegar

1 cup (240 ml) water

2 cups (384 g) sugar

½ cup (120 g) salt

½ tbsp (3 g) coriander seeds

1 tsp juniper berries

4 oz (120 g) carrots, julienned

4 oz (120 g) daikon radish, julienned

HOT AND SWEET SAUCE
1 (28-oz [840-ml]) bottle Sriracha sauce

¼ cup (60 ml) soy sauce

1½ cups (360 ml) honey

Zest and juice of 1½ limes

LAMB
1 (3-lb [1.35-kg]) full lamb breast

4 oz (120 g) coarse kosher salt

8 oz (240 g) raw sugar

8 oz (240 g) coarsely ground black pepper

4 (6- to 8-inch [15- to 20-cm]) French baguettes

Butter, as needed

2 oz (60 g) fresh cilantro leaves, stems removed

To make the pickled daikon and carrots, combine the distilled white vinegar, rice wine vinegar, water, sugar, salt, coriander seeds and juniper berries in a large pot over medium-high heat. Bring the mixture to a boil and cook for 5 minutes, making sure the sugar and salt have dissolved. Place the carrots and daikon in a large heatproof bowl and pour the boiling mixture over them. Let the mixture cool and refrigerate it for 24 hours.

To make the hot and sweet sauce, combine the Sriracha, soy sauce, honey and lime zest and juice in a medium bowl and whisk until it's blended. Keep the sauce refrigerated.

To make the lamb, peel the back off the lamb breast. Combine the salt, sugar and pepper in a bowl. Season both sides of the breast liberally with the salt mixture. Set up your smoker to cook indirectly and smoke the lamb for 9 hours at 250°F (121°C), or until the meat pulls off the bone. Pick all the meat from the breast. Be sure to discard any cartilage and silver skin.

Split the baguettes and butter the insides. Toast the baguettes on the hot grill. Remove them from the heat and put some hot and sweet sauce on both sides. Lay 6 ounces (180 g) of smoked lamb on the bottom of the sandwich, then place 3 ounces (90 g) of pickled daikon and carrots on top of the lamb. Finish by dividing the cilantro among the sandwiches on top of the pickled vegetables. Serve immediately.

KOREAN STICKY RIBS

One of the items that really stood out for me at Hometown Bar-B-Que were the Korean Sticky Ribs. Frying the ribs for ten seconds really changes the texture, while adding the Korean sauce takes the flavor profile to the next level.

COOK TIME: 4 hours   **YIELD:** 1 rack (10 to 12 bones)

KOREAN SAUCE

1 tbsp (15 ml) sesame oil

1½ tbsp (14 g) minced fresh garlic

2 tsp (6 g) minced fresh ginger

1 lb (450 g) light brown sugar

2 cups (480 ml) tamari

⅔ cup (160 ml) water

¼ cup (60 ml) rice wine vinegar

¼ cup (60 ml) Korean pepper paste or gochujang

1 tsp freshly ground black pepper

¼ cup (38 g) cornstarch combined with ¼ cup (60 ml) cold water

RIBS

4 oz (120 g) coarse kosher salt

1 lb (450 g) raw sugar

1 (2½- to 3-lb [1.1- to 1.4-kg]) rack baby back ribs, peeled and trimmed

½ cup (120 ml) canola oil

4 scallions, finely chopped

4 oz (120 g) fried garlic

4 oz (120 g) fried shallots

4 oz (120 g) raw cashews, coarsely chopped

To make the Korean sauce, heat the sesame oil in a medium pot over low heat. Add the garlic and ginger and cook for about 1 minute.

Add the brown sugar, tamari, water, vinegar, pepper paste and black pepper. Increase the heat to medium and bring the sauce to a simmer.

Once the sauce begins to simmer, add the cornstarch mixture. Remove the pot from the heat when the sauce starts to boil. Set the sauce aside.

To make the ribs, mix the salt and sugar together in a large bowl.

Coat both sides of the ribs with the salt rub and shake to remove any excess rub. Let the rub sit on the ribs for 30 minutes before smoking.

Smoke the ribs at 250°F (121°C) for approximately 4 hours, or until the ribs are tender. The cook time will vary based on the smoker.

Cut the rack into individual ribs.

In a large skillet, heat the canola oil to 350°F (177°C). Add the ribs and fry them for 10 seconds to crisp the outside.

Drain the excess oil and add the Korean sauce to the skillet. Toss to coat the ribs.

Top the ribs with the scallions, fried garlic, fried shallots and cashews.

SAM JONES BBQ

715 W. Fire Tower Rd.
Winterville, NC 28590
www.samjonesbbq.com

Third-generation pitmaster Sam Jones is serving up the best eastern Carolina barbecue you can find. Sam's grandfather, the late Pete Jones, opened the Skylight Inn in the summer of 1947. Skylight is still in operation today and overseen by Sam, his dad and his uncle. Since the doors opened, Skylight has served whole-hog pork, corn bread and coleslaw. As Sam traveled, he saw other forms of barbecue and wanted to make those items when he returned home. But he knew if he did it at Skylight, it would take away from the tradition instead of add to the restaurant's allure. So in 2016, with the help of his friend and business partner Michael Letchworth, Sam opened Sam Jones BBQ.

I met Sam at the Big Apple Barbecue Block Party and quickly realized he is the Mark Twain of barbecue. His stories have a feeling of realism of place and language, portray memorable characters and are characterized by a broad irreverent humor and social satire. During my brief time as a wallflower among the barbecue elite, I heard Sam say something that I hold close: "A legacy does not have an impact if it is unrealized." He is a proud man, proud of what his forefathers have created and proud to be able to share that with others throughout the world. As irony would have it, in addition to overseeing two successful barbecue joints, Sam is also the fire chief for Ayden, North Carolina. And he realizes that the same fire that can be destructive can also create something wonderful.

Sam Jones BBQ is a beautiful restaurant. The outside of the restaurant resembles an old warehouse and the smokehouse is right beside it. A trip to Sam Jones BBQ wouldn't be complete if you didn't order the Jones Family Original BBQ tray (barbecue pork, slaw and corn bread). The pork served here is on an entirely different level than what you might have ever experienced. The tray of chopped pork consists of different cuts of meat and pieces of crunchy skin. The little pieces of skin provide a texture that really sets Sam Jones BBQ apart. The barbecue is great just as it's served, but I also tried their East N.C. Sweet Heat BBQ Sauce. The slaw is sweet and the corn bread tastes like it's been rendered down with the hog. I also had some turkey, ribs and baked beans. All items were championship-barbecue quality.

BARBECUE BAKED BEANS

Sam Jones's whole hogs are legendary; however, no Southern barbecue is complete without a side. Sam Jones's baked beans are savory enough to stand on their own but also complement any protein you pair them with. I found that the addition of ground beef makes this a particularly savory dish.

COOK TIME: 57 minutes   **YIELD:** 12 to 15 servings

1 tbsp (15 ml) vegetable oil

½ large green bell pepper, seeds and ribs removed, diced

½ large white onion, peeled, trimmed and diced

12 oz (360 g) 80/20 ground beef

2 (28-oz [840-g]) cans pork and beans, drained

1½ cups (360 ml) ketchup

½ cup (72 g) brown sugar

1½ tbsp (24 g) yellow mustard

Preheat the oven to 350°F (177°C).

Heat the oil in a medium skillet over medium heat. Add the green bell pepper and onion and cook for about 5 minutes. Add the ground beef, stir and cook for 7 minutes, or until the beef is crumbled and is no longer pink.

In a 13 x 9–inch (33 x 23–cm) baking dish, combine the beef mixture with the pork and beans, ketchup, brown sugar and mustard. Stir to fully combine. Bake for about 45 minutes.

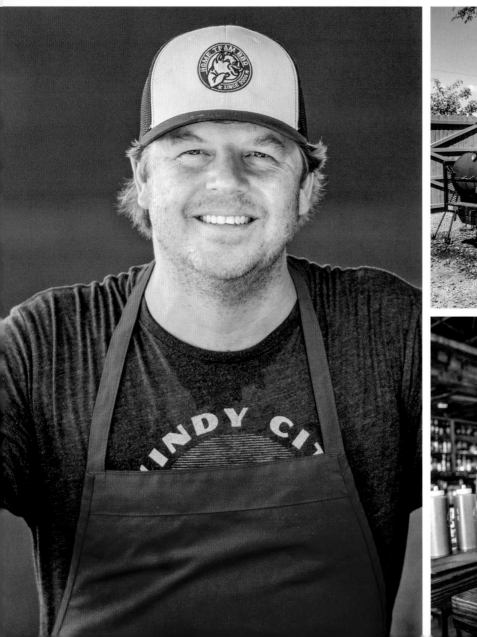

126 Williman St.
Charleston, SC 29403
www.hometeambbq.com

Home Team BBQ has become an institution in South Carolina, with three locations (Sullivan's Island, West Ashley and downtown Charleston). Home Team BBQ has also opened a location in Aspen, Colorado, and another South Carolina location, this time in Columbia, is in the works.

After graduating from the University of Georgia, Aaron Siegel moved to New York to attend The Culinary Institute of America. It was during his spare time at the institute that he started to mess around with barbecue and eventually got bitten by the barbecue bug.

In 2006, Aaron partnered with Taylor Garrigan, Tony McKie and Madison Ruckel to open Fiery Ron's Home Team BBQ in West Ashley. A few years later, they expanded and opened another location on Sullivan's Island, followed by downtown Charleston and Aspen in 2016.

It takes one taste of the food at Home Team BBQ to answer any question on how they were able to grow. Their smoked chicken wings with white sauce are fantastic. From the pork cracklings to the smoked turkey to the Brunswick stew, I knew why Home Team BBQ was voted best barbecue by the public every year since 2008. You must order the chopped brisket taco. The flavor was out of this world—ten minutes after eating, I wanted to run back and get more.

BEEF RIBS WITH ADOBO

There is no bigger wow factor at a dinner table than to set out a tray of short ribs. They are the biggest, meatiest beef ribs, usually sold in three-bone portions. This creation that Aaron Siegel came up with is an absolute show stopper. Your guests will be talking for days about this meal.

COOK TIME: 10 to 12 hours   **YIELD:** 6 to 8 servings

ADOBO

10 guajillo chiles

Boiling water, as needed

2 whole cloves

½ tsp cumin seeds

1 (½-inch [13-mm]) cinnamon stick

1 tsp dried Mexican oregano

6 cloves garlic

½ cup (120 ml) fresh orange juice

¼ cup (60 ml) apple cider vinegar

1 tbsp (9 g) light brown sugar

2 tsp (12 g) kosher salt

RIBS

2 (5-lb [2.2-kg]) 3-bone beef ribs

1 oz (30 g) kosher salt

2 tbsp (12 g) freshly ground black pepper

To make the adobo, remove the seeds and stems from the *guajillo* chiles. Heat a large cast-iron skillet over high heat for 2 to 3 minutes. Place the chiles in the hot skillet and stir them with tongs until wisps of smoke begin to appear, about 5 minutes.

Remove the chiles from the skillet and place them in a large heatproof bowl. Cover the chiles with the boiling water and let them soak for at least 30 minutes. Remove the chiles from the water and reserve the chiles and water separately.

Heat the same cast-iron skillet over high heat for 2 to 3 minutes. Add the cloves, cumin seeds, cinnamon stick and Mexican oregano and toast the spices for 2 to 3 minutes. Remove them from the skillet and let cool for 10 minutes. Place them in a spice grinder and process until a powder is formed. Reserve the spice mixture.

Heat a small cast-iron skillet over high heat for 2 to 3 minutes. Add the garlic to the skillet and toast it for 3 to 4 minutes.

In a blender, combine the rehydrated chiles, spice mixture, garlic, orange juice, vinegar, brown sugar and salt. Blend the ingredients until the mixture is smooth, using the reserved chile water as needed to help the blender process.

To make the ribs, prep a smoker to 225°F (107°C). Remove the membrane from the bone side of the beef ribs. Evenly distribute the salt and pepper on the surface area of the beef ribs. Place the ribs on the smoker bone side down. Smoke the beef ribs at 225 to 250°F (107 to 121°C) until an internal temperature of 190°F (88°C) is reached, 10 to 12 hours.

Brush the ribs with the adobo and let them rest to a temperature of 150°F (66°C). Remove the bones (they should pull out easily) and remove any cartilage from the bone side of meat. Slice across the grain and serve with the remaining adobo.

CHARRED CORN ESQUITES

Esquites, or Mexican street corn salad, is a savory side dish that you won't be able to get enough of. Esquites is the off-the-cob version of *elotes*, Mexican street corn that's grilled and then slathered with condiments including salt, mayonnaise, cheese, chili powder and lime. Esquites is delicious and easy to customize to your taste.

COOK TIME: 10 to 12 minutes   **YIELD:** 6 to 8 servings

CORN

8 medium ears fresh corn

2 tbsp (30 ml) canola oil

2 tbsp (36 g) kosher salt

1 tbsp (6 g) freshly ground black pepper

DRESSING

1 tsp minced fresh garlic

1 tbsp (13 g) minced fresh jalapeño

¼ cup (12 g) coarsely chopped scallions

1 tbsp (3 g) fresh cilantro, coarsely chopped

1 tbsp (15 ml) fresh lime juice

¼ cup (55 g) mayonnaise

½ cup (90 g) Cotija cheese

1 tsp chili powder

1 tsp ground Espelette

1 tsp kosher salt

½ tsp freshly ground black pepper

Prepare a charcoal grill to cook directly at 325°F (163°C).

To make the corn, shuck the ears of corn and remove any remaining threads with a kitchen towel. In a large bowl, combine the oil, salt and pepper and evenly distribute the oil mixture on the corn.

Grill the corn for 10 to 12 minutes, until it is slightly charred and cooked through. Chill the corn and remove the kernels from the cobs with a sharp knife. Reserve the corn kernels.

To make the dressing, combine the garlic, jalapeño, scallions, cilantro, lime juice, mayonnaise, Cotija cheese, chile powder, Espelette, salt and pepper in a large bowl. Mix thoroughly with a wooden spoon. Add the dressing to the corn kernels and stir to distribute the dressing evenly. Esquites can be made in advance and kept in the refrigerator for 2 to 3 days.

801 Jerry Clower Blvd. N.
Yazoo City, MS 39194
www.ubonsbbq.com

If you look up "Southern hospitality" in the dictionary, there should be a picture of Ubons BBQ of Yazoo City. Pronounced "you-bahns," this family restaurant is everything that barbecue ever was, is and is supposed to be: family, good food and good times. There is no smile in barbecue greater than a Roark smile, and you are sure to be greeted with one when you enter the door of Ubons.

This father-daughter team has made Ubons BBQ a nationally recognized brand. From participating at some of the nation's most prestigious barbecue events to cooking a private dinner at the James Beard Foundation, the Roark family has never forgotten their Delta roots. Ubon Roark, Garry's father and Leslie's grandfather, was the son of a southeast-Missouri farmer. His family was known for their summer barbecue tradition. Ubons Barbeque Sauce, served and sold today, is Ubons's original recipe and goes back at least five generations. In addition to barbecue sauce, the Roark family also has a Bloody Mary mix that is one of the best on the market.

Ubon passed his cooking gene down to Garry, who passed it on to Leslie. Leslie would become the first female to ever win the Memphis in May World Championship Barbecue Cooking Contest. In 2003, this dynamic duo opened Ubons BBQ restaurant in their hometown of Yazoo City, Mississippi. Today you can find Jacob and Ellie Mae, Leslie's son and daughter, at the restaurant, learning the family traditions of generations past.

Unsurprisingly, the food is just as amazing as the hospitality—the pulled pork was some of the best I had on my tour. The Ubons crew is eclectic, as is their menu. When I visited they had a specials board for the day that had items such as barbecue tamales, a catfish platter and a Bloody Mary cucumber salad. I am a sucker for a good cucumber salad—it is nostalgic for me, as my grandmother would always have a bowl of cucumber salad on the table. The salad was a perfect complement to our pulled pork. It was refreshing and the combination of Bloody Mary mix and vinegar struck the perfect balance.

Unfortunately, shortly after our most recent visit to Ubons, word spread of the untimely passing of Garry Roark. He was a man with a heart larger than barbecue. He was a true gentleman and could tell a joke to make you laugh yourself off your chair. I recall my last conversation with Garry: Leslie, Jacob and the Ubons team had just cooked a private dinner at the James Beard House in New York. He was so proud talking about his family and the Yazoo City community. I hope one day people see the same sparkle in my eye when I talk about my family.

BLOODY MARY CUCUMBER SALAD

Leslie recalls the huge garden her grandparents used to have at their home in the country. Each time she visited them during the summer, Mamaw would have a cucumber salad ready. It was this memory that inspired Leslie to create a great summertime salad for your family.

PREP TIME: 10 minutes   **YIELD:** 8 servings

2 large cucumbers, peeled and thinly sliced

2 medium tomatoes, finely chopped

1 large Vidalia onion, diced

1 cup (340 g) shredded cabbage (optional)

½ cup (96 g) sugar

⅔ cup (160 ml) Ubons Bloody Mary Mix (PitMaster's Hot and Spicy or BBQ)

⅔ cup (160 ml) apple cider vinegar

2 tbsp (6 g) finely chopped fresh dill

2 tbsp (6 g) finely chopped fresh basil

Salt, to taste

Freshly ground black pepper, to taste

In a large bowl, combine the cucumbers, tomatoes, onion, cabbage (if using), sugar, Bloody Mary mix, vinegar, dill, basil, salt and pepper. Stir to distribute the ingredients. Serve chilled.

1238 DeKalb Ave. NE
Atlanta, GA 30307
www.foxbrosbbq.com

Growing up in Texas, twin brothers Jonathan and Justin Fox didn't have to look far for inspiration to make great barbecue. Jonathan and Justin taught themselves how to cook. Fox Bros. Bar-B-Q originated like most great barbecue joints do—in the backyard. Jonathan and Justin would invite friends and family over to enjoy the great food coming off their pit. Before they knew it, there was live music and more than two hundred people showing up to their place. "I've always loved having parties and being able to feed all of my friends and family," says Jonathan.

Today, Fox Bros. Bar-B-Q is an Atlanta fixture, earning top spots on barbecue rankings nationwide. With fresh renovations to their flagship restaurant, Fox Bros. Bar-B-Q continues to serve Atlanta's favorite barbecue to their extensive fan base. The laid-back barbecue joint is located on DeKalb Avenue, across from the train tracks in a predominantly residential area. However, there is no missing the all-red building with the Fox Bros. Bar-B-Q logo on it. Guests have an option to sit inside or they can enjoy the beautiful Atlanta climate outside on the patio. Due to Jonathan and Justin's success, it's not uncommon for customers to double-park in the parking lot and to inform the hostess of who they are blocking in case someone needs to leave. When I was there I heard at least a few license plate numbers being called out by the hostess.

Jonathan and Justin are lauded as having the best barbecue in Atlanta, and after eating there I wouldn't limit their prowess to the city limits. This is some of the best barbecue you will have anywhere.

SMOKED CHICKEN WINGS

The wings at Fox Bros. Bar-B-Q are insane. They are smoked over hickory and then flash-fried for tender and crisp wings. The wings are then tossed in a spicy sauce that will tame but not overwhelm the smokiness. While this version isn't fried, I'm sure you'll enjoy it just as much as if you were eating at Jonathan and Justin's restaurant.

COOK TIME: 2½ hours **YIELD:** 4 servings

DRY RUB
1½ cups (180 g) paprika

1¼ cups (432 g) kosher salt

¾ cup (90 g) chili powder

½ cup (60 g) granulated garlic

½ cup (60 g) granulated onion

½ cup (55 g) freshly ground black pepper

3 to 4 tbsp (27 to 36 g) cayenne pepper (optional)

WINGS
24 jumbo fresh chicken wings, rinsed and cleaned

1½ cups (360 ml) barbecue or wing sauce (preferably Fox Bros. brand), divided

To make the dry rub, combine the paprika, salt, chili powder, granulated garlic, granulated onion, black pepper and cayenne pepper, if using, in a large bowl. Mix well. Store the dry rub, covered, in a dark place.

Prepare your smoker to cook between 225 and 250°F (107 and 121°C).

To make the wings, combine the wings and 1 cup (120 g) of the dry rub in a large bowl. Make sure the wings are evenly coated with the rub.

Place the wings on the smoker evenly, with some space between them. Smoke the wings for 2½ hours. Flip the wings halfway through the smoking time to give them even exposure to the smoke. Remove the wings from the smoker.

If you like your wings dry, they are ready to eat. If you like them saucy, put ¾ cup (180 ml) of the barbecue sauce in a medium bowl. Add 12 of the wings and toss to coat the wings in the sauce. Transfer the sauced wings to a serving plate and repeat this process with the remaining ¾ cup (180 ml) of barbecue sauce and 12 wings. Add more sauce to your liking if desired.

TIP: *When making wings on a smoker, you may not get that crispy skin you are accustomed do. A barbecue tip from the Devil: Add 2 tablespoons (22 g) of baking powder to your rub. Baking powder is composed of an acid that draws moisture to the surface of the chicken skin, where it evaporates, accelerating the browning process so your chicken can get nice and crispy.*

HOMEMADE RUB ARSENAL

A rub allows each pitmaster to develop a proprietary and iconic flavor profile. From sweet and spicy to savory and traditional, the combinations are endless. There are countless commercial rubs that are great to use at home. Most of the recipes supplied by the pitmasters in this book contain rubs that they produce and sell to use at home. For those looking to make their own flavor profile, try one of these rub recipes as your starting point.

THE DEVIL'S BASE RUB

This is my classic dry rub base. The turbinado sugar and paprika add texture and color to your bark.

YIELD: 1½ cups (240 g)

½ cup (60 g) paprika

¼ cup (63 g) turbinado sugar

¼ cup (72 g) kosher salt

¼ cup (30 g) granulated garlic

2 tbsp (12 g) coarsely black pepper

1 tbsp (9 g) onion powder

1 tsp cayenne pepper

1 tsp chili powder

Combine the paprika, sugar, salt, granulated garlic, black pepper, onion powder, cayenne pepper and chili powder in a small bowl. Store the rub in an airtight container for up to 6 months.

COFFEE RUB

This makes for a savory blend that tastes great on steaks, hamburgers and beef ribs.

YIELD: 1 cup (120 g)

½ cup (144 g) kosher salt

3 tbsp (6 g) dark roast ground coffee

2 tbsp (12 g) coarsely ground black pepper

1 tbsp (15 g) turbinado sugar

½ tsp chili powder

½ tsp cocoa powder

Combine the salt, coffee, pepper, sugar, chili powder and cocoa powder in a small bowl. Store the rub in an airtight container for up to 6 months.

"PLEASE TELL ME" RUB

Every time I use this rub, someone asks for the recipe. It's great on poultry and seafood, and it can even jazz up your veggies.

YIELD: ½ cup (60 g)

2 tbsp (18 g) sweet Hungarian paprika

1 tbsp (18 g) coarse-flake salt

1 tbsp (9 g) chipotle chile powder

1 tbsp (9 g) granulated garlic

1½ tsp (3 g) freshly ground black pepper

1½ tsp (5 g) ground thyme

1 tsp ground rosemary

Combine the paprika, salt, chipotle chile powder, garlic, pepper, thyme and rosemary in a small bowl. Store the rub in an airtight container for up to 6 months.

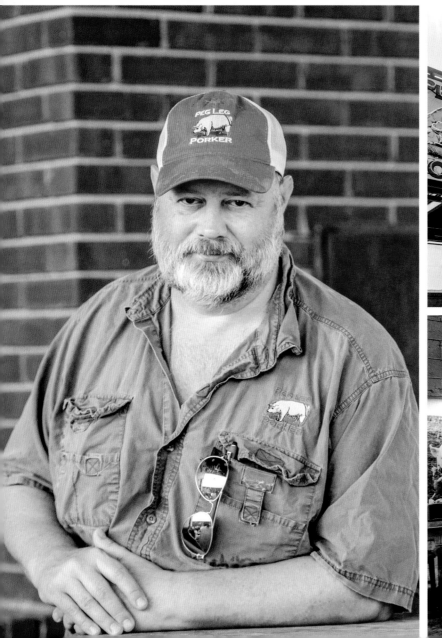

903 Gleaves St.
Nashville, TN 37203
www.peglegporker.com

It would be tough to find anyone serving traditional Tennessee barbecue better than Carey Bringle and the staff at Peg Leg Porker. The ribs are a quintessential Tennessee dry ribs, smoked only with kosher salt and then topped with a dry seasoning. The Bringle family has been a part of Covington, Tennessee, since the early 1800s. To Carey, it is important to stick to the barbecue he grew up with: traditional barbecue pork and chicken. No beef here. As Carey would say, "If you want brisket, go to Texas."

At seventeen, right before his senior year of high school, Carey lost his right leg after a fight with bone cancer. Carey is a fun-loving guy who will tell you, "Either you mope around or you fight and move forward." His enthusiasm for life and sense of humor is echoed throughout his brand, Peg Leg Porker. While he likes to have fun, Carey is serious when it comes to barbecue competition. In 2016, Carey's Peg Leg Porker team won third place in the whole-hog category at the Memphis in May World Championship Barbecue Cooking Contest.

Carey wants you to feel like you're at home when you visit his Peg Leg Porker restaurant. And trust me, you'll feel the tradition when you walk in. The entire restaurant is filled with images of the Bringle family and their story. While other barbecue joints are opening multiple locations, Carey is fine with one place. This is his family, his home, and he wants to share it with you. Great food, great atmosphere and great people: Peg Leg Porker is a must-stop whenever you're in Nashville.

SMOKED GREEN BEANS

As I sat to talk with Carey, he brought a tray of ribs and green beans to the table. As I expected, the ribs lived up to the hype of prior reviews, but it was the green beans that really caught my eye. I grew up in a farming family—we had green beans three times a week, but these were different. They were smoky, savory and full of flavor. I had to ask Carey what his secret was. When Carey makes his beans, he has a few racks of ribs on the shelf above at the same time. The beans catch the drippings and infuse that pork goodness into the cooking process.

COOK TIME: 3 hours   **YIELD:** 10 to 12 servings

3 lb (1.3 kg) fresh green beans, trimmed and chopped into 1-inch (2.5-cm) pieces

2 cups (480 ml) water

2 tbsp (30 ml) apple cider vinegar

¼ large onion, cut into slivers

4 oz (120 g) bacon, coarsely chopped

2 tsp (4 g) freshly ground black pepper, or to taste

1 tsp salt, or to taste

In a large baking dish, combine the green beans, water and vinegar. Add the onion, bacon, pepper and salt. Place the baking dish in a smoker, uncovered, and smoke for 3 hours.

PEG LEG PORKER BBQ SAUCE

This is a base sauce meant to be tailored to your taste. It is a start to get you going on your barbecue adventures. For example, you can add a dry seasoning, such as Peg Leg Porker BBQ Seasoning or your favorite rub, to make it your own.

YIELD: 3 cups (720 ml)

2 cups (480 ml) ketchup

¼ cup (60 ml) apple cider vinegar

¼ cup (36 g) brown sugar

⅛ cup (30 g) yellow mustard

¼ cup (60 ml) honey

In a medium bowl, combine the ketchup, vinegar, brown sugar, mustard and honey. Refrigerate until ready to use.

THE SHED BBQ AND BLUES JOINT

OCEAN SPRINGS, MISSISSIPPI   »   BRAD ORRISON AND BROOKE ORRISON LEWIS

Ocean Springs, MS 39565

www.theshedbbq.com

You'll be hard-pressed to find a more creative environment than The Shed BBQ and Blues Joint. In 2001, Brad and his sister, Brooke Orrison Lewis, opened the doors to a tiny 300-square-foot (28-sq.-m) barbecue takeout on Highway 57 in Ocean Springs, Mississippi. There was a good reason they named their barbecue joint The Shed. Self-admittedly, Brad was a collector: Old tin roofing, used windows, discarded wood—you name it, he probably had it. When it came time to build his vision, Brad and Brooke knew where they could find the building supplies. Over the years, The Shed has developed into roughly 10,000 square feet (929 sq. m) of pure creative fun. I wouldn't classify The Shed as a restaurant, because it's way more than that. It's a destination, entertainment for the whole family and an experience like none other. From the moment you arrive in the parking lot, you'll know you're not in Kansas anymore. There are multiple seating options indoors and out, a stage where some of the finest blues can be heard and other numerous creative uses of the space along the bayou, including an elevated ramp walkway to the restrooms. As you watch others visit The Shed, it's difficult to tell who's enjoying their time more—the adults or the children.

The Shed is a prime example of a family-run business. While Brad is always coming up with new and creative ideas, Brooke is overseeing the business side of his creations. Brother Brett is the sound engineer for the blues joint, making sure they remain one of the finest blues venues in the South. Mama Mia handles the marketing for The Shed and Daddy-O oversees their barbecue sauce production. The Orrisons will tell you that their place is "a family stage—their outlet to the world, a place all are welcome as long as they are looking for a good time."

While the atmosphere and attitude might be laid-back at The Shed, the barbecue is 100 percent serious business. The Shed has won numerous awards for their barbecue, including their second world championship most recently at the 2018 Memphis in May World Championship Barbecue Cooking Contest. In addition to the championship, they also took home top honors in the chicken-wing, whole-hog and Kingsford Tour of Champions categories.

I tried a Shed Sampler Platter, consisting of wings, ribs, brisket, sausage, chicken and a few sides. It was all fantastic and probably the only thing that could keep me from wandering around.

BACON-WRAPPED AND BOUDIN-STUFFED PORK TENDERLOIN

Like most barbecue pitmasters, Brad is resourceful. Not only in collecting the eclectic display of local artifacts that give The Shed its namesake, but also in using local ingredients to make great culinary dishes. He shared with me a recipe for a pork tenderloin stuffed with boudin. Boudin is a regional specialty found only in southern Louisiana. This scrumptious treat is traditionally made with pork, rice, seasonings and various vegetables, such as onions and green peppers. There are many unique recipes because each New Orleans butcher prepares the sausage in a different way, so the varieties are endless.

COOK TIME: 45 minutes   **YIELD:** 4 servings

1 (1-lb [450-g]) pork tenderloin

1 lb (450 g) Compart Duroc brand applewood-smoked bacon

¼ cup (30 g) The Shed Brisket Rub, divided

1 cup (220 g) duck fat, divided

½ lb (225 g) boudin sausage

½ lb (225 g) triple-cream Brie cheese

¼ cup (30 g) The Shed Rib Rub

Place the tenderloin on a cutting board. Using a sharp knife, make a ¼-inch (6-mm) long cut on the flattest part of the loin. Filet the loin into a flat sheet—do not trim the edges.

Using the bacon, make a bacon weave as large as you can, keeping the slices very tight together in the pattern.

Season one side of the loin with ⅛ cup (15 g) of the The Shed Brisket Rub. Flip the loin over and place it on top of the bacon weave. Coat the loin with ½ cup (110 g) of the duck fat. Lightly season the other side of the loin with the remaining ⅛ cup (15 g) of The Shed Brisket Rub.

Remove the boudin from its casing, leaving it in a sausage form. Cut the triple-cream Brie into 1-inch (2.5-cm) logs and mold the boudin and Brie into a round log.

Wrap the loin around the boudin-Brie stuffing, rolling tightly until you have reached the end. Coat the outside of the roll with the remaining ½ cup (110 g) of duck fat and season the roll with The Shed Rib Rub. Trim the ends of the loin evenly to ensure the bacon will surround the entire loin.

Prepare the smoker to cook indirectly at 275 to 300°F (135 to 149°C). Place the roll on the smoker and cook for 45 minutes, until the meat reaches an internal temperature of 145°F (63°C). Once the desired temperature is reached, remove the roll from the smoker and let it rest for 8 minutes. In order to crisp the bacon weave, cook the roll with direct heat for a few minutes on each side, making sure the bacon doesn't curl up. Slice and serve.

DADDY-O'S LIVE FIRE CAJUN BBQ SHRIMP

What trip to the Delta would be complete without a Cajun shrimp recipe? This one comes from Daddy-O Orrison himself. Grilled local shrimp on toasted garlic French bread. Yeah, buddy!

COOK TIME: 15 minutes   **YIELD:** 6 servings

1 lb (450 g) fresh shrimp, size 21/25 count or larger

Salt, as needed

Freshly ground black pepper, as needed

⅓ cup (50 g) diced red onion

⅓ cup (50 g) diced Vidalia onion

½ cup diced bell pepper (any color)

⅓ cup (50 g) diced celery

4 tbsp (60 g) unsalted butter

2 tbsp (6 g) fresh parsley, finely chopped

2 tbsp (30 ml) Worcestershire sauce

Vermouth, as needed

Juice of 1 lemon

¼ cup (30 g) The Shed Rib Rub

1 French baguette

¼ cup (38 g) minced garlic

Peel and devein the shrimp and place them on ice to ensure freshness. Skewer the shrimp and season them with salt and pepper.

Set up the smoker to cook directly at approximately 325°F (163°C).

In a large skillet over the smoker's fire, sauté the red onion, Vidalia onion, bell pepper and celery for 3 minutes. As the onions start to become translucent, add the butter and parsley and sauté for 3 to 5 minutes. Add the Worcestershire sauce, a splash of vermouth, the lemon juice and The Shed Rib Rub. Bring the mixture to a slow boil and cook for 3 minutes.

Grill the shrimp lightly for approximately 2 minutes on each side and add them to the sauce (do not overcook the shrimp).

Meanwhile, slice the baguette through the middle horizontally. Grill the baguette for 2 minutes and add the garlic while it is toasting. During this time, you can tent the skillet, allowing smoke to enter and exit freely, if extra smoke flavor is needed. Slice each half of the baguette into thirds. Top the bread with the shrimp and spoon any remaining au jus from the skillet over the shrimp.

ALL HAIL THE KING

464 N. Nassau St.
Charleston, SC 29403
www.lewisbarbecue.com

John Lewis is a Texas native. He grew up in El Paso and moved to Austin when he was eighteen to pursue a culinary career. In 2009, he helped Aaron Franklin open Austin's most famous barbecue joint, Franklin Barbecue. A couple years later, he partnered with LeAnn Mueller as the pitmaster at la Barbecue in Austin. It wasn't until John made a visit to Charleston to cook with legendary Rodney Scott that he decided he wanted to live there. In 2015, John packed up his world-class brisket recipe and his offset smokers and headed 1,250 miles (2,011 km) east.

What some might not realize is that John is an accomplished pit builder as well as pitmaster. When John was at la Barbecue, he worked on an offset smoker that would make a brisket to his liking. With the help of his father and roughly five different design builds, John assembled the pieces of his pit with precise dimensions. The smokehouse at Lewis Barbecue was the most impressive and awe inspiring on our tour: four 1,000-gallon (3,785-L) propane tanks converted into beautiful offset smokers.

Upon entering Lewis Barbecue, you are immediately greeted at the service counter where brisket and sausages are being sliced in front of you. With ample seating inside and a courtyard area between the main dining room and smokehouse, everything is visually appealing at Lewis—from the food to the surroundings. The brisket at Lewis is arguably the best you will ever have. In addition to the brisket, order a few Texas Hot Guts (housemade sausage links) when you go.

HATCH GREEN CHILE CORN PUDDING

My favorite side at Lewis Barbecue was the Hatch Green Chile Corn Pudding. Corn pudding has been a Southern staple for years, and it's an especially popular addition to Thanksgiving menus. But this is John Lewis's corn pudding, a dish that rivals the pitmaster's beef ribs and brisket in the acclaim category. Its well-balanced texture and subtle chili flavor make the cheesed pudding suitable for just about any occasion

COOK TIME: 30 minutes   **YIELD:** 8 servings

¼ cup (31 g) all-purpose flour

¼ cup (43 g) yellow cornmeal

2 tbsp (24 g) sugar

1 tsp kosher salt

½ tsp baking powder

¼ tsp granulated garlic

3 large eggs

⅔ cup (160 ml) heavy cream

8 oz (240 g) frozen corn, thawed and pureed

¼ cup (43 g) finely chopped roasted Hatch green chiles

4 oz (120 g) mild cheddar cheese, cut into ½-inch (13-mm) cubes

¾ cup (130 g) fresh corn kernels

2 tbsp (30 g) butter

¼ cup (30 g) shredded mild cheddar cheese

Combine the flour, cornmeal, sugar, salt, baking powder and granulated garlic in a medium bowl and stir until the mixture is homogeneous.

In a large bowl, beat the eggs and whisk in the heavy cream. Add the corn puree, Hatch green chiles, cubed cheddar cheese and fresh corn kernels.

Pour the flour mixture into the egg mixture. Whisk until the batter is homogeneous.

Preheat the oven to 375°F (191°C), with a medium cast-iron skillet in the oven.

Take the heated cast-iron skillet out of the oven and add the butter. Allow the butter to heat until it is foaming and the milk solids are lightly toasted, about 2 minutes. Be sure to allow the butter to fully coat the bottom of the skillet. Pour the corn pudding batter into the hot cast-iron skillet with the foaming butter. Sprinkle the shredded cheddar cheese on top of the batter and return the skillet to the oven.

Cook the pudding for 30 minutes. The cheese should be nicely browned and the pudding should be set but not firm in the center. Allow the pudding to rest for 5 minutes and serve.

TRUTH BARBEQUE

BRENHAM, TEXAS　»　LEONARD BOTELLO IV

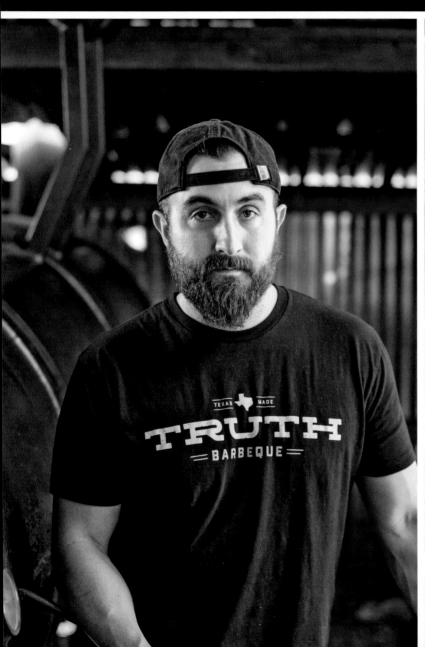

2990 US 290
Brenham, TX 77833
www.truthbbq.com

Leonard Botello IV and his family opened Truth Barbeque in 2015. Their primary marketing tool was word of mouth. And the word traveled fast. In just two years, they turned their roadside barbecue joint into *Texas Monthly* magazine's top ten best barbecue joints in the state.

Located between Austin and Houston, Leonard will admit there isn't much to see in Brenham. However, if there's good barbecue, people will find it. While Leonard grew up working in his family's restaurant, it wasn't barbecue. Instead, he purchased a used Klose barbecue pit and started studying. From the local influences of Aaron Franklin and John Lewis to social media and YouTube posts, Leonard developed knowledge and a direction for his barbecue business.

Let the truth be known that the restaurant is a family affair: On a typical day, you can find Leonard slicing up your order while his dad gets your sides and rings up your order. Leonard's mom, Janel, makes all the homemade cakes on the Truth Barbeque dessert menu.

It's apparent that Leonard's studies paid off—with the help from some post oak smoke, he can turn a prime brisket into a masterpiece. Equally amazing were the ribs and turkey that I enjoyed. For my sides, I enjoyed the pinto beans with rib meat and collard greens.

Truth Barbeque is opening its second location in Houston, Texas. Leonard assured me that the same quality barbecue provided at Brenham will be served at the larger Houston location. I have no doubt it will be, and I can't wait to visit when the new location opens.

SMOKED WINGS WITH CILANTRO RANCH

The great thing about chicken wings is the diversity in flavor profiles you can experiment with. The variety of rubs and finishing sauces allow you to use a tried-and-true cooking process and develop a unique product every time. These smoked wings are a great alternative to the "traditional" Texas Trinity (brisket, ribs and sausage) while still getting to use your smoker. I love these for fun dinners, game days, parties or even staff snacks when we're prepping for a big event at the restaurant.

COOK TIME: 2 hours   **YIELD:** 4 servings

24 bone-in chicken wings

Salt, as needed

Freshly ground black pepper, as needed

2 cups (480 ml) Truth Hot Sauce or Louisiana brand hot sauce

4 tbsp (60 g) butter

1 clove garlic

1 (16-oz [480-ml]) bottle ranch dressing

2 cups (32 g) fresh cilantro

Celery sticks, for serving (optional)

Carrots, for serving (optional)

Season the raw chicken wings with salt and pepper and set them aside.

In a food processor, puree the hot sauce, butter and garlic. Transfer the hot sauce to a medium bowl.

Combine the ranch dressing and cilantro in the food processor. Pulse until the ingredients are blended. Transfer the cilantro ranch to a small bowl and chill until you are ready to serve.

Set up your barbecue to cook indirectly at 250°F (121°C). Cook the wings until they reach an internal temperature of 175°F (79°C), approximately 2 hours.

Once the wings have reached the desired internal temperature, transfer them to a large bowl and toss them in the hot sauce. Serve the wings with a side of chilled cilantro ranch and celery and carrots, if desired.

TIP: *For a juicier wing, french the wings prior to cooking them and tossing them in the sauce. French cuts separate the meat and skin from a portion of the bone. The meat sits on one end of the wing piece and the exposed bone presents itself as a neat "handle" for easy gripping. Use a sharp knife to saw through the skin at the thin bottom of the drumette. Work around the entire bottom, stopping once the skin seems completely disconnected there. Use the side of the knife blade to push the meat down from the thin end of the bone and farther onto the thick end of the bone.*

HOLIDAY SMOKED PRIME RIB

I don't know about you, but there are some years when I feel like doing something other than turkey or ham for the holidays. If you grew up like I did, you might be wondering what other choices there are. But I have to admit that one of my most favorite holiday turkey alternatives is prime rib. It is the choicest of beef cuts. Rich, tender, elegant—but still a traditional family dish. So come holiday time, prime rib might just be that perfect traditional, but unexpected, main dish you've been looking for to grace your family table.

COOK TIME: 2 hours   **YIELD:** 4 servings

1 (4- to 6-lb [1.8- to 2.7-kg]) prime rib roast

Yellow mustard, as needed

1½ tbsp (23 g) salt

2 tbsp (12 g) freshly ground black pepper

5 cloves garlic, minced

1 tbsp (3 g) minced fresh thyme, plus more for garnish

1 tbsp (3 g) minced fresh rosemary, plus more for garnish

8 tbsp (120 g) unsalted butter

Let the rib roast come to room temperature (which may take 45 to 60 minutes). Once the roast is at room temperature, coat it with a thin layer of mustard. Season the roast with the salt and pepper.

In a small bowl, combine the garlic, thyme and rosemary. Gently pat the mixture onto the roast.

Place the roast in a medium chef's pan and cook in an indirect-heat grill (such as charcoal) at a constant 275°F (135°C) until the internal temperature of the roast is 120°F (49°C), approximately 2 hours. When the meat reaches an internal temperature of 100°F (38°C), place the butter in a small chef's pan in the smoker. Once the meat reaches an internal temperature of 110°F (43°C), baste the roast with the melted butter. Do this in a continuous manner with a large spoon, the way you might with a cast-iron steak, constantly ladling butter over the entire roast.

When the roast has reached 120°F (49°C), remove it from the smoker, wrap it loosely in foil and let it sit for 30 minutes. This will allow the juices to redistribute through the roast. When you're ready to serve, garnish the roast with additional thyme and rosemary and cut it into 1-inch (2.5-cm) thick slices.

MARTIN'S BAR-B-QUE JOINT

NASHVILLE, TENNESSEE » PAT MARTIN

410 4th Ave. S.
Nashville, TN 37201
www.martinsbbqjoint.com

Pat Martin will tell you it was his family that got him into barbecue: "I got into grilling because of my dad. He loved barbecue. That, and I was born in Memphis, so it's in my DNA." For Pat, it's important to pass along what he's learned to keep this tradition alive. It's also the reason why, when his company grows, it's not without him having his hands on every part of a new store. "The only way I can grow is to teach these guys how to do it themselves," he says. "It's not recipe driven. It's a skill set."

Walk into any of his eight barbecue joints (five in Tennessee, two in Kentucky and one in Alabama), and the first thing you smell and feel is the smoke. My visit took me to the downtown Nashville location, where four whole-hog pits running 24/7 are the sources of the tantalizing smell throughout the entire 13,000-square-foot (1,207-sq-m) establishment. The downtown Nashville location is a pitmaster's dream: It is massive, it is beautiful and it is my version of heaven—a former warehouse turned into a multilevel barbecue palace with more things to see and do during your stay than you can imagine. This place is a destination. The barbecue is world-championship status and so are the staff and environment. The sound of large fans circulating the wonderful aroma and the pitmasters tending to the whole hogs make you feel as though you are in another world.

All the food looked too good not to try. So undo the belt a notch and order a Big Daddy Sampler: ribs, pork, brisket, chicken and 3 pints (1.4 L) of sides. Trust me, it will fill up a family of four, no problem. Before I left, Pat greeted me with something I don't see too often in the North: a smoked bologna sandwich and a side of broccoli salad. I didn't think I could eat anything more until I tried and subsequently finished the sandwich and salad.

SMOKED AND FRIED BOLOGNA SANDWICHES

Being from the Northeast, I've never had to the opportunity to make fried bologna a part of my diet. Then Pat explained the process and I was hooked—he had me at "rubbed," "smoked" and "fried." The 1-inch (2.5-cm) slabs of fried bologna are matched up wonderfully with the yellow mustard, onion and pickle. These are great sandwiches for the tailgating crowd—make sure you pair them with a nice lager.

COOK TIME: 4 hours   **YIELD:** 20 servings

1 (10- to 12-lb [4.5- to 5.4-kg]) whole bologna log

¼ cup (30 g) Martin's Bar-B-Que Joint's Big Hoss Rub

½ cup (120 ml) canola oil

Loaf of white bread

1 (12-oz [360-ml]) bottle yellow mustard

1 (16-oz [480-ml]) jar Wickles Dirty Dill Chips pickles

1 large sweet onion, cut into ¼-inch (6-mm) thick slices

Starting a day before you'd like to serve the sandwiches, light your smoker or grill to cook indirectly at 250°F (121°C). Place the cold bologna log on a cutting board and, using a chef's knife, score three ½-inch (13-mm) deep cuts on the log. Rotate the log and score it 3 more times. Rotate the log a final time and score it 3 final times.

Lightly dust the bologna with the Big Hoss Rub. Place the bologna on the smoker for about 3½ hours. Place the bologna on a large baking sheet and place it, uncovered, in the refrigerator for at least 6 hours, preferably overnight.

Remove the bologna from the refrigerator and slice it into 1-inch (2.5-cm) thick slices. If you will not be using all the bologna, you can wrap the unused portion and freeze it for later.

Pour the oil into a medium cast-iron skillet and place the skillet over medium-high heat. Using tongs, carefully place the bologna slices in the skillet, being careful not to splatter the oil and or overcrowd the skillet. Fry the bologna for about 2 minutes, then, using tongs, carefully flip the slices and cook the other sides for about 1 minute. The bologna should be lightly crisp. Transfer the slices to a paper towel to drain.

Place 2 slices of bread on a plate. Spread about 1 tablespoon (15 ml) of mustard on 1 slice of bread. On the mustard, place 1 pickle at each corner. On the other slice of bread, place a slice of bologna then top it with 4 or 5 slices of onion.

BROCCOLI SALAD

When it comes time to throw a barbecue for my family and friends, I tend to overlook the sides. While proteins will always be the star of the show, I find it important to accompany them with something complementary and unique. The broccoli salad by Martin's is a well-balanced salad that is easy to make, tastes great and will get rave reviews—a great alternative to macaroni or potato salad.

PREP TIME: 10 minutes   **YIELD:** 12 servings

4 to 6 cups (365 to 545 g) fresh broccoli florets

¾ cup (113 g) diced red onion

¾ cup (90 g) shredded sharp cheddar cheese

¾ cup (165 g) crumbled bacon

¾ cup (114 g) raisins

1 cup (240 ml) Martin's Bar-B-Que Alabama White Sauce

1 tbsp (14 g) mayonnaise

In a large bowl, combine the broccoli, onion, cheddar cheese, bacon and raisins. In a small bowl, whisk together the Martin's Bar-B-Que Alabama White Sauce and mayonnaise. Pour the dressing over the broccoli salad and toss to coat. Cover the bowl and refrigerate for at least 1 hour before serving.

BARBECUE SLANG 101

TALK LIKE A PITMASTER

The barbecue brethren have their own language, a slang of coded words that, unless you've worked at a barbecue joint, will sound bizarre to you. If you attend a barbecue festival or talk to a pitmaster, you may hear some of the following barbecue terms.

BARK

The flavorful outer layer of large cuts of barbecue meat.

BOSTON BUTT

The upper part of the shoulder of a hog's front leg. Most commonly used to make pulled pork.

FAT CAP

A thick layer of fat between the skin and meat, found on briskets and pork butts.

MONEY MUSCLE

Located high on the Boston butt pork shoulder, the money muscle is moist and flavorful. The easiest way to locate the money muscle is to find the bone and go to the opposite side. When cooked properly, it is melt-in-your-mouth goodness. It's what gets the calls from judges and is known for putting the pitmaster in the money.

PITMASTER

The title bestowed on barbecue society's highest order. Through time and trial, these heroes preside over hot coals to create slow-smoked proteins of greatness.

POINT

The fatty part of the brisket, also known as the deckle or nose.

SHIGGIN

When pitmasters spy on their competition, trying to learn their secrets.

SHINERS

Bones that are exposed on a rack of ribs. The bones "shine" through the meat. Shiners should be avoided at all times.

SMOKE RING

The smoke ring is produced by a chemical reaction between the pigment in the meat and the gases produced by wood or charcoal. When combined with myoglobin, a protein found in the meat, a coveted pink hue called the smoke ring appears just underneath the bark.

STALL OR PLATEAU

When cooking brisket or Boston butts, the meat's internal temperature will reach 165°F (74°C), then stall. After two or three hours, the meat's temperature will start to rise again.

17TH STREET BARBECUE

MURPHYSBORO, ILLINOIS » MIKE AND AMY MILLS

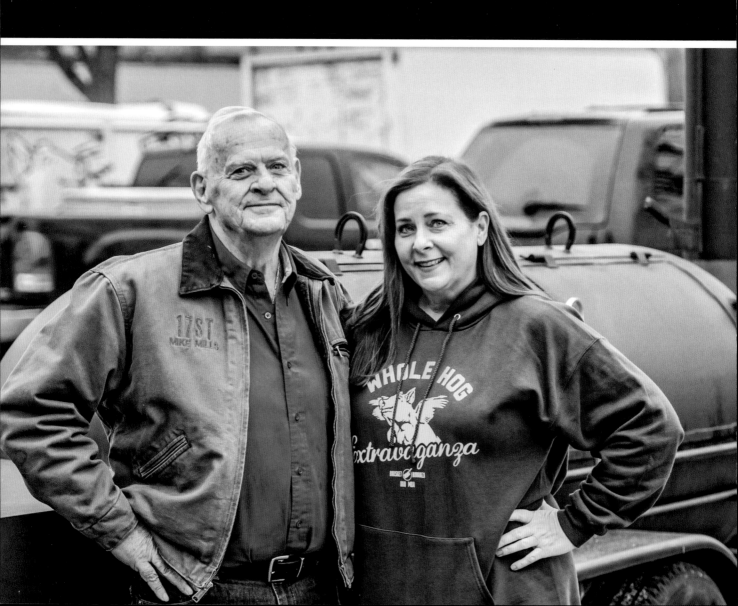

32 N. 17th St.
Murphysboro, IL 62966
www.17bbq.com

Throughout this book, you will hear me discuss the brethren of barbecue, the family-like atmosphere among pitmasters nationwide. There are no two names more affectionately synonymous with sharing the passion of barbecue than Mike and Amy Mills. In fact, pitmasters and chefs from forty-five states and fifteen countries have flocked to Murphysboro, Illinois, for the past few years at the invitation of Mills and his daughter Amy for the ultimate barbecue learning experience: the Whole Hog Extravaganza Brisket Bonanza MBA. Over the course of three days, Mike Mills and pitmasters from across the country teach the intricacies of their craft to those in attendance.

Mike Mills, fondly referred to as "The Legend," presides over pits at seven nationally acclaimed barbecue restaurants in Illinois and Las Vegas and serves as a partner at Blue Smoke restaurant in New York City. He has won the world champion title four times and the grand world champion title three times at the Memphis in May World Championship Barbecue Cooking Contest. He also won grand champion at the Jack Daniels World Championship Invitational Barbecue. Mike and Amy have authored two books, *Peace, Love, and Barbecue* and *Praise the Lard.*

At the corner of 17th and Elm in Murphysboro sits the big brick and metal building of barbecue lore. The food is everything you would expect to have at the house of barbecue royalty. The menu boasts so many delicious things, you will face never-ending decisions. However, there are some staples to the menu that 17th Street is known for: their ribs, pork steak and Lotta Bull brisket sandwich to name a few. But 17th Street is more than just traditional barbecue. Always looking for a way to keep the barbecue scene vibrant, the Millses are always creating new and exciting items. Make sure you check out their specials when you visit.

PEACH HAND PIES

Amy was fond of a recipe they came up with for peach hand pies. If there's anything better than a homemade pie, it's a petite and crusty hand pie that you can claim as your own and nibble on at your leisure.

COOK TIME: 18 to 20 minutes   **YIELD:** 12 hand pies

CRUST

2½ cups (313 g) all-purpose flour, plus more as needed

1½ tsp (6 g) sugar

1 tsp kosher salt

8 tbsp (120 g) cold unsalted butter, cubed

½ cup (115 g) cold lard

5 tbsp (75 ml) ice water

FILLING

4 cups (225 g) sliced ripe fresh peaches, cut into ½-inch (13-mm) cubes

2 tbsp (24 g) granulated sugar

1 tbsp (9 g) light brown sugar

1 tsp ground cinnamon

1 tbsp (6 g) grated lemon zest

1 tbsp (15 ml) fresh lemon juice

1 large egg

1 tbsp (15 ml) water

Sparkling sugar or granulated sugar, for sprinkling

To make the crust, combine the flour, sugar and salt in a food processor and pulse to mix. Add the butter and lard and pulse gently until the mixture resembles coarse crumbs. Drizzle in the water, 1 tablespoon (15 ml) at a time, and pulse just until the mixture forms a dough.

Transfer the dough to a work surface. Divide the dough in half and shape it into 2 balls. Flatten the balls into disks, wrap the disks separately and chill them for 1 hour.

Preheat the oven to 400°F (204°C) with a rack in the center. Line a large baking sheet with parchment paper.

To make the filling, place the peaches in a large bowl. Add the granulated sugar, brown sugar, cinnamon, lemon zest and lemon juice and combine.

Whisk the egg and water together in a small bowl to make an egg wash.

Lightly flour a work surface and roll out 1 disk of pie dough into a 14-inch (35-cm) circle about ⅛ inch (3 mm) thick.

Using a round cookie cutter or a saucer, cut out six 6-inch (15-cm) circles of dough.

Divide half of the peach filling among the 6 circles, mounding the filling on one side of each circle. Brush the egg wash on the edge of the circles. Fold each pie crust over the filling, pressing gently to seal and using a fork to crimp the edges. Repeat this process with the second disk of pie dough and the remaining peach filling.

Brush the top of each pie crust with egg wash and sprinkle it with the sparkling sugar.

Cut a slit in the top of each pie to allow steam to release and arrange the pies on the prepared baking sheet. Bake the hand pies on the center rack for 18 to 20 minutes, until golden brown.

Transfer the hand pies to a wire rack to cool.

HOLY CITY HOGS

Ravenel, SC
www.holycityhogs.com

Pitmasters will cook on various pits, use various woods to smoke with and have countless rubs and sauces at their disposal. However, the one thing that each great pitmaster starts with is a high-quality product. Tank Jackson and Holy City Hogs have established a reputation for quality hogs that far exceeds their small town of Ravenel, South Carolina. His hogs are highly sought after by legendary pitmasters of Nashville as well as an NYC chef doing a private dinner for *GQ* magazine.

When I visited Charleston, I decided to touch base with Tank and see if he had a few minutes to share with me what makes Holy City Hogs so special. The mission at Holy City Hogs is to provide premium-quality pork for America's top chefs, restaurants and discerning individuals. The operation specializes in raising Ossabaw Island and American Mulefoot hogs, along with many other heritage breeds, helping ensure these wonderful ingredients will be on tables for generations to come. Tank knows swine, and with his full beard, long hair and trucker hat, he fits the part. If you're a hog, Holy City Hogs is the Club Med of hog farms. The large farm is made up of woods and open fields, which allow the hogs to feed and live in their natural habitat. Tank is well aware of what his hogs eat. "We feed a mix of local grains and culled seasonal fruits and veggies as well as the forage in their natural habitats," he explains. Tank feels allowing his hogs to live and eat in their natural environment gives his hogs an advantage over his competitors' animals.

As we were talking about the Charleston food scene, Tank made mention of the time he worked in the kitchen as a pastry chef. Tank stated, "My great grandma and grandma taught me to make desserts and I was raised by a Cherokee woman who taught me how to cook. Her name was Rose. I named my daughter after her." In addition to making some great desserts, Tank is also making some great sausage. If you ever see Holy City Hogs sausage on the menu, order it.

PEANUT BUTTER PIE

I admit that I have a huge sweet tooth. At each stop along my barbecue tour, I made sure to save room for dessert. There are a ton of desserts that originated south of the Mason-Dixon line, many of which you've likely tried. However, if someone ever offers you an icebox pie, take them up on it. I don't care how good the pecan pie or banana pudding looks, an icebox pie is a slice of home. When I asked Tank for a recipe, I specifically asked for an icebox pie. He replied, "Really, it's pretty simple." But then again, isn't all barbecue pretty simple? Meat, spice and fire are all you need. I hope you enjoy Tank's version of an icebox pie.

YIELD: 16 servings

8 tbsp (120 g) butter

2 (8-oz [240-g]) packages cream cheese

2 cups (260 g) powdered sugar

1 (32-oz [960-g]) jar crunchy or smooth peanut butter

1 (8-oz [240-g]) container whipped topping

2 store-bought graham cracker or chocolate cookie pie crusts

¼ cup (45 g) peanut butter morsels

¼ cup (45 g) chocolate chips

Allow the butter and cream cheese to soften at room temperature for 30 to 60 minutes. With a stand mixer, blend together the butter, cream cheese and powdered sugar. Add the peanut butter. After a malleable texture is reached, fold in the whipped topping by hand. Divide the filling between the 2 pie crusts. Sprinkle the peanut butter morsels and chocolate chips on top of the pies. Place the pies in in the refrigerator for short-term storage at least 30 to 45 minutes before serving or in the freezer for long-term storage.

TRUDY'S UNDERGROUND BARBECUE

STUDIO CITY, CALIFORNIA » BURT BAKMAN

8136 W. 3rd St.
Los Angeles, CA 90048
www.trudysundergroundbarbecue.com
www.slabbarbecue.com

As the name suggests, this barbecue is underground—you've got to track down pitmaster Burt Bakman to get an invitation to one of his cookouts, or contact him for orders. Prior to the opening of his new restaurant, Slab, unless you were a friend of Bakman, the only way to get some of his highly sought-after Trudy's Underground Barbecue was through social media direct messaging.

Bakman's path to barbecue fame might be the longest traveled among all the pitmasters featured in this book. It wasn't until he was teenager that his family moved to the States. Los Angeles, as a matter of fact—not really the barbecue capital of the world. Prior to coming to the United States, Burt spent time in Germany and Israel. Even at a young age, he was intrigued with cooking, learning the cultural techniques and tastes of each stop. It wasn't until Bakman made a trip to Texas for an unrelated purpose that he fell in love with the flavor profile of Texas barbecue. When he returned home, it was time to replicate its characteristics while developing his own flavor profile. His popularity soon rose as he went from making one or two briskets a weekend to ten. That's when Burt decided to make a substantial investment and purchase a FatStack Smoker. Now he would be able to make more than forty briskets at a time—but he'd never cooked on an offset this size. Welcome to the bond and brethren of the barbecue community. Bakman reached out to Leonard Botello IV of Truth Barbeque in Texas, who shared his knowledge with Burt.

Those who are unable to get an invite to the Studio City location need not worry much longer. Burt Bakman is moving into a retail space of his own, thanks to the restaurant-focused h.wood Group team. You might say it was barbecue destiny. One day, Bakman was out delivering his food to a friend, who brought some to Brian Toll of the h.wood Group. Toll loved it and the rest is history. The new location will be on 3rd Street in Los Angeles and named Slab BBQ.

BRISKET BENEDICT

Burt has created a breakfast recipe that will not only make use of that extra brisket but elevate your breakfast to a new level.

COOK TIME: 12 to 14 minutes   **YIELD:** 6 servings

12 large eggs, divided

1¼ cups (288 g) butter, divided

3 large egg yolks

2 tbsp plus 1 tsp (35 ml) fresh lemon juice

1½ tsp (5 g) brisket rub

Pinch of ground Aleppo pepper, plus more as needed

6 English muffins, split

1 lb (450 g) coarsely chopped fatty point brisket

Kosher salt, to taste

Freshly ground black pepper, to taste

2 tsp (2 g) finely chopped fresh chives

Fill a large pot three-quarters full with water and bring it to a gentle simmer over medium-low heat. Place a large bowl of ice water near the stove. Working one at a time, crack 6 eggs into a fine-mesh sieve set over a small bowl and shake the sieve gently to allow the more liquid part of the egg white to pass through and discard. Gently transfer each egg to a medium bowl, being careful not to break the protective ring of egg white surrounding the yolk. Once you have 6 strained eggs in the bowl, gently position the bowl over the pot of simmering water and, one at a time, slip each egg into the pot. Cook the eggs, gently encouraging each to rotate with a slotted spoon so they cook evenly, until the whites are set and the yolks are still runny, 3 minutes. Skim off and discard any foam or bits of egg white in the pot. Return the water to a gentle simmer. Repeat this poaching process with the remaining 6 eggs.

Heat the butter in a medium saucepan over low until melted. Set aside ¼ cup (60 ml) of the melted butter. Transfer the remaining butter to a small liquid measuring cup. Remove any milk solids that come up to the surface to clarify the butter.

Fill a blender pitcher with very hot water and let it sit 3 minutes to warm the blender pitcher—this will prevent the sauce from separating. Drain the pitcher; dry it well. Blend the egg yolks and lemon juice in the blender just to combine them. With the blender motor running, slowly stream in the melted butter in the liquid measuring cup until the hollandaise sauce is thick, glossy and a pale yellow. Transfer the hollandaise sauce to a medium bowl; stir in the brisket rub and Aleppo pepper. Taste and adjust the seasonings, if needed. If sauce seems too thick, thin it with 1 to 2 tablespoons (15 to 30 ml) of warm water and adjust the seasonings as needed.

Preheat the oven to 450°F (232°C). Arrange the English muffins, cut side up, on a medium baking sheet. Brush them with the reserved ¼ cup (60 ml) of melted butter. Toast the muffins until they are golden brown around the edges, 6 to 8 minutes. Divide the brisket among the muffins. Place 1 poached egg atop the brisket. Season the eggs with salt and black pepper. Spoon the hollandaise sauce over the eggs. Top with the chives and additional Aleppo pepper.

THE SALT LICK BBQ

DRIFTWOOD, TEXAS » SCOTT ROBERTS

18300 Farm to Market Rd. 1826
Driftwood, TX 78619
www.saltlickbbq.com

Take a forty-minute drive out of Austin, Texas, and you will find The Salt Lick BBQ in Driftwood. Since 1967, the Roberts family has been serving up some of the most popular Texas barbecue. The trip to The Salt Lick symbolizes everything you've ever thought Texas barbecue would be. Grass-lined highways with the occasional sighting of cows and horses, then a trip down a winding back road and you are at a barbecue joint the size of Texas. It's impressive with a large building for weddings and events, an on-site winery and an ATM (The Salt Lick is cash only). For the barbecue aficionado, it's difficult not to sprint to the entrance once your feet hit the gravel parking lot.

Upon entering The Salt Lick, you're immediately greeted by their iconic giant pit: piles of meat on top of the grill, all kinds of sausage hanging from the top and post oak burning into the most mesmerizing smell. For those with an insatiable appetite or who are unsure what to have, The Salt Lick offers a family-style plate—for $25 you get all-you-can-eat beef brisket, sausage, pork ribs, potato salad, coleslaw and beans. After a couple days of eating brisket, I wanted a change of pace and ordered some bison ribs and turkey and couldn't have been happier with my decision. The bison ribs were remarkable; they were the back ribs, not the huge beef short ribs you might be accustomed to seeing. They were glazed and left on the pit for just the right amount of time to let the sauce set. The coleslaw was the surprise of the day. The taste of celery and sesame seed was something I didn't expect. It was a great variation of a barbecue classic. Then it was time for dessert and the abundance of pecan pies in the restaurant had me drooling from the start; however, when I ordered dessert, the words "peach cobbler" came out of my mouth. I think my brain knew something my stomach didn't, because the peach cobbler was excellent. This was the best dessert on my Texas tour.

Pro tip: Pack a cooler, as The Salt Lick is BYOB friendly. If you are traveling from Austin, hit one of the local breweries for supplies (I highly recommend Hi Sign Brewing, Live Oak Brewing Company, Independence Brewing Company and The ABGB). If you need a snack for the ride to Driftwood, stop by Voodoo Doughnuts—only $1.05 for a quality, delicious doughnut. I love Texas.

SMOKED TURKEY BREAST

A smoked turkey is the perfect full-flavored, low-fat centerpiece to your holiday buffet. The unique flavor of this moist, tender meat and the ready-to-serve convenience make it a wonderful holiday meal. Use fresh turkey whenever you can—we have found that with frozen turkeys, there is a tendency for the breast meat to dry out (see Tip).

COOK TIME: 5½ hours   **YIELD:** 12 servings

POULTRY BRINE
24 cups (5.8 L) water

1 cup (192 g) sugar

½ cup (120 g) salt

TURKEY BREAST
1 (12-lb [5.4-kg]) turkey breast

1 (12-oz [360-ml]) bottle The Salt Lick Original BBQ Sauce

To make the poultry brine, combine the water, sugar and salt in a large, airtight container.

To make the turkey breast, rinse the turkey breast and pat it dry. Seal it in the large container with the poultry brine and place the container in the refrigerator for 24 hours.

Bring the smoker to 265°F (129°C). When you are ready to smoke, rinse the brined turkey with cold water and pat it dry. Baste the turkey well with The Salt Lick BBQ Sauce. Place the turkey on the smoker rack midway from the heat source. Baste the turkey after 3 hours. At 5½ hours, check the internal temperature of the turkey at the thickest area of the breast. If the temperature is 165°F (74°C), the turkey breast can be removed from the smoker. If the internal temperature is not 165°F (74°C), check it every 15 minutes.

Remove the turkey breast from the smoker and place it on a large baking sheet to rest. Baste the turkey before slicing and serving.

TIP: *To combat the possibility of a dry bird, place 2 pats of butter between the skin and the meat on each breast.*

COLESLAW

Coleslaw might be the quintessential side dish when you think of barbecue. Just as barbecue is regional, so are the side dishes. This no-mayonnaise recipe from The Salt Lick BBQ includes sesame and celery seeds for a unique flavor profile.

PREP TIME: 20 to 25 minutes **YIELD:** 12 servings

1½ cups (360 ml) distilled white vinegar

½ cup (96 g) sugar

⅛ cup (30 g) salt

⅛ tsp ground white pepper

1 large head cabbage, shredded

⅛ cup (30 ml) vegetable oil

Pinch of celery seeds

1 oz (30 g) sesame seeds, toasted

Place the vinegar in a heavy medium saucepan over medium-high heat and bring it to a boil. While the vinegar is boiling, slowly add the sugar and salt, stirring constantly until they have dissolved. Turn off the heat. Place the white pepper in a medium bowl. Slowly pour the vinegar mixture over the white pepper while whisking to combine them. Cover the bowl.

Place the cabbage in a large bowl. Drizzle the oil over the cabbage and mix thoroughly. Sprinkle the celery seeds and sesame seeds on top of the cabbage and mix thoroughly. Add the vinegar mixture and combine well. Transfer the coleslaw to a serving bowl, scraping all the remaining seeds and dressing from the large bowl and adding them to the serving bowl. Serve immediately—this coleslaw is best served while the cabbage is crisp.

See the image on page 90.

A CRASH COURSE ON CHARCOAL AND WOOD

Before you light the cooker, it's important you realize that charcoal is for heat and wood is for flavor. Unless you are using a pellet-fueled smoker, gas grill or stick burner, charcoal will be your heat source. Your wood will provide your food the barbecue flavor you desire while working in tandem with your charcoal. The types of charcoal and wood are a personal preference. Making good barbecue is all about consistency of time, temperature and smoke. I prefer natural lump charcoal over briquettes due to the ease of lighting and the higher temperature lump charcoal will allow you to cook at. Also, I use only wood chunks or cut pieces rather than wood chips.

There are typically two classifications of wood: light and hard. Light woods are typically from fruit-bearing trees. Harder woods can burn hotter, burn longer and have a more noticeable smoke flavor. It is important to take into consideration what you are cooking when deciding which wood to select. Poultry and seafood are a sponge for smoke, so you'll want to select a light wood. On the other hand, larger bulk cuts of meat will embrace all the hickory and oak you can give them.

APPLE

The most common of light woods, apple provides a subtle fruit flavor and color. Apple works well with pork and chicken.

CHERRY

Cherry is a great wood for pork and poultry. Cherry creates a beautiful color to your pork while adding a sweet-tasting smoke flavor. I use cherry for all my competition pork and chicken products.

HICKORY

A popular hardwood that lends a heavier smoke flavor to the food you are cooking. Goes well with pork and beef.

MESQUITE

A dominant smoke-flavor hardwood. Use a little mesquite initially until you develop a flavor profile you are happy with.

OAK

You will hear of most Texas barbecue joints using either hickory or post oak. Oak is a subtler version of hickory. It can burn hot and it can burn long. Oak has a great smoke flavor and pairs well with beef.

PECAN

A great all-around light wood. A sweet and mild flavor that will also put a nice color on your meat.

PEACH

Similar to cherry, peach is a wood that is great for seafood and white meats. It has a smoke flavor profile similar to hickory, just much lighter.

BBQ BOB TRUDNAK AND MOE CASON

MONTGOMERY COUNTY, PENNSYLVANIA

www.bbqguru.com

www.moecasonbbq.com

Robert "BBQ Bob" Trudnak has been grilling and smoking professionally for more than fifteen years. He has won more than two hundred awards and prizes at national and international barbecue competitions, including the title of grand reserve champion at the Jack Daniels World Championship Invitational Barbecue. BBQ Bob is also an entrepreneur and inventor, having helped launch an entire line of the world's first high-tech cooker accessories for BBQ Guru, a leading designer and manufacturer of innovative barbecue equipment. These include the award-winning PartyQ, DigiQ and CyberQ Cloud automatic temperature control devices.

BBQ Bob is passionate about helping others learn the joy of barbecuing by teaching cooking classes in both the United States and Europe. He also runs a family-owned catering business, Hav'N a BBQ, and is the creator of competition-winning sauces and rubs.

Ponderosa Barbeque Team is the name of Moe Cason's one-man championship barbecue team out of Des Moines, Iowa. He has participated in twenty contests every year since 2006, bringing his total to more than 250 competitions to date. Moe Cason is a self-taught pitmaster dedicated to the craft of barbecue who embraced the skills and knowledge of cooking passed down by his mother and grandmother. Moe is one of the larger-than-life personalities on the barbecue circuit. From his trademark "lil' blue" pit, overalls and cigar to his patriotic smile when talking about his family, his military service or old Mopar cars, Moe is a great ambassador for barbecue.

Moe and Bob offer some of the best rubs and sauces used in the backyard and on the Kansas City Barbeque Society (KCBS) competition circuit. Visit their respective sites for more information on how to get your hands on some.

I met up with Bob and Moe at the New Jersey State Barbecue Championship™ in Wildwood. While they were busy amassing numerous competition awards, they found time to make me a Philly pork sandwich on the new Monolith BBQ.

PHILLY PORK SANDWICH
WITH BROCCOLI RABE, GRILLED LONG HOTS AND SHARP PROVOLONE

When most of us think of a Philadelphia meat and cheese sandwich, the first thing that comes to mind is a cheesesteak. But for those who hail from the City of Brotherly Love, the pork sandwich served for family dinner on Sunday will consist of pork, broccoli rabe and provolone. These sandwiches are great for tailgating, concerts or a picnic in the park. You can make them ahead of time, wrap them in foil and place them in an empty cooler. When you arrive at your destination you can enjoy them immediately while your neighbors get jealous.

COOK TIME: 9 hours   **YIELD:** 6 servings

1 (8- to 10-lb [3.6- to 4.5-kg]) Hatfield brand pork butt

BBQ Bob's Alpha Rub, as needed

BBQ Bob's 7Bones Rub, as needed

4 tbsp (60 ml) olive oil, divided

1 tsp red pepper flakes

Kosher salt, as needed

2 large bunches broccoli rabe

10 oz (300 g) sharp provolone cheese

12 Italian long hot peppers

6 hoagie rolls

Set up the barbecue to cook indirectly at 275°F (135°C) with the wood of your choice (oak and cherry work well for this recipe). Season the pork butt with a moderate dusting of BBQ Bob's Alpha Rub, then a light top layer of BBQ Bob's 7Bones Rub. Smoke the pork butt for approximately 9 hours, or until the internal temperature reaches 204°F (96°C). Pull the meat and set it aside. Keep the drippings from the pork and separate the fat.

In a large pot over medium heat, combine 2 tablespoons (30 ml) of the olive oil, red pepper flakes and salt. Remove the leaves and heavy stems from the broccoli rabe and sauté them in the olive oil for approximately 12 minutes, or until the broccoli rabe becomes tender. Meanwhile, coarsely chop the provolone cheese.

In a large skillet, heat the remaining 2 tablespoons (30 ml) of olive oil over medium-high heat. Add the Italian long hot peppers and cook them for 4 to 6 minutes. Flip the peppers and cook for 4 to 5 minutes, until the skins are light brown in color. Let the peppers cool until they can be handled. Remove the skins and seeds and gently chop them into bite-size pieces.

To assemble a sandwich, use tongs to grasp some of the pulled pork, dip the pork into the hot pork drippings and place the pork on a hoagie roll. Top the pork with some broccoli rabe, then some Italian long hots. Top the Italian long hots with some provolone cheese and serve.

BLUE SMOKE

NEW YORK, NEW YORK » JEAN-PAUL BOURGEOIS

116 E. 27th St.
New York, NY 10016
www.bluesmoke.com

Step inside Blue Smoke and you will momentarily forget you're in the flatiron district of midtown Manhattan. Blue Smoke is a barbecue joint with a woody barroom full of red-vinyl booths, a skylight-lit dining room and a jazz club downstairs. With the help and guidance of Mike and Amy Mills, famous restaurateur and St. Louis native Danny Meyer opened Blue Smoke in 2002. Executive Chef Jean-Paul Bourgeois continues to make Blue Smoke a leader by offering a variety of dishes that complement all regions of American barbecue.

Chef Bourgeois draws inspiration from his native Louisiana, serving soulful Southern barbecue and sides like five pepper brisket, smoked chicken wings with Alabama white sauce and corn bread madeleines. Trained for fine dining, Chef Bourgeois makes it his mission to represent and revive the cuisine of his kin and that of all Southerners. He strives to honor and celebrate the traditions of Southern cooking and cultures that came before us through sustainable food and new-world techniques.

I hit the bustling midtown location at lunchtime and was seated promptly. Chef Bourgeois was gracious enough to greet me and spend some time talking about the state of barbecue before the duties of a busy kitchen called him. It was lunch, so I was going to take it easy: cornbread madeleines, chicken wings, tri-tip with salsa verde and creamed spinach. Thankfully, Sean Ludwig from NYC BBQ joined me for lunch to hear about my travels. First to hit the table were the madeleines and wings. The wings, served with an Alabama white sauce, might have been the best wings I've ever had. The madeleines felt so delicate with their thin outer crust, yet they packed a ton of flavor in a small package. The tri-tip was smoked perfectly and the salsa verde was indescribable. I found myself putting it on everything. Jean-Paul's creamed spinach is as good as that at any Michelin-rated steakhouse.

Whether you're in NYC for lunch or dinner or you're looking for some world-class jazz, do yourself a favor and stop at Blue Smoke, a flatiron location where you can enjoy some award-winning Southern cuisine and barbecue in an intimate and comfortable environment.

GRILLED SCALLION SALSA VERDE

Salsa verde is a spicy green sauce in Mexican cuisine. It is based on tomatillo and chile pepper. You might not think of salsa verde as a barbecue item, but this jalapeño and Aleppo pepper recipe from Chef Bourgeois is a great topping for any red meat coming off your grill.

COOK TIME: 10 minutes   **YIELD:** 8 cups (2 L)

20 bunches scallions

4 large jalapeños, divided

8 cloves garlic, grated

1 cup (240 ml) olive oil

1 cup (240 ml) neutral-flavored oil (such as canola or vegetable)

½ cup (20 g) packed fresh parsley, coarsely chopped

½ cup (20 g) packed fresh cilantro, coarsely chopped

1 tbsp (9 g) ground Aleppo pepper

Red wine vinegar, to taste

Zest of 2 oranges

Zest of 2 lemons

Salt, to taste

Freshly ground black pepper, to taste

Grill the scallions over low heat until they are charred, approximately 2 minutes per side, cooking the whites first, then the greens so the scallions are evenly cooked. While the scallions are grilling, grill 3 of the jalapeños until they are charred, approximately 4 minutes per side. Once the jalapeños are cool enough to handle, peel and dice them. Finely dice the remaining jalapeño, along with its seeds.

Once the scallions are cool, chop them coarsely and add them to a large bowl along with the garlic, charred jalapeños, olive oil, neutral-flavored oil, parsley, cilantro and Aleppo pepper. Gently stir until combined, making sure not to bruise the herbs. Season to taste with the vinegar, orange zest, lemon zest, salt and pepper right before serving to prevent discoloration.

CREAMED SPINACH

Chef Bourgeois shares a part of his family tradition with a recipe from his mamaw. This recipe is for a delicious and cheesy creamed spinach. It's easy and tastes much better than any store-bought version. It may not be a traditional barbecue side dish, but I have found this recipe pairs well with poultry and red meat.

COOK TIME: 30 to 32 minutes   **YIELD:** 4 servings

8 tbsp (120 g) unsalted butter

2 oz (60 g) finely chopped yellow onion

1 tbsp (9 g) minced garlic

1 dried bay leaf

1 lb (450 g) chopped frozen spinach

1 (8-oz [240-g]) package cream cheese

½ tsp ground Aleppo pepper

½ tsp freshly ground black pepper

Salt, to taste

In a medium skillet over medium heat, melt the butter while constantly scraping the bottom to remove the brown bits. Cook the butter until it is golden brown, 2 minutes. Discard the bay leaf. Add the onion, garlic and bay leaf. Cook for 8 to 10 minutes, or until the onion is soft. Add the spinach. Cover the skillet and cook for 5 minutes to help thaw the spinach without burning the bottom.

Once the spinach is mostly thawed, uncover the skillet and continue to stir the spinach mixture for 10 minutes, or until most of the liquid has evaporated. Add the cream cheese, Aleppo pepper and black pepper. Cook until the cream cheese is melted and dispersed through the entire mixture, 5 minutes. Season the creamed spinach with salt to taste.

SWIG & SWINE

CHARLESTON, SOUTH CAROLINA » ANTHONY DIBERNARDO

1217 Savannah Hwy.
Charleston, SC 29407
www.swigandswinebbq.com

When I started putting together my list of must-stops for this book, a former classmate reached out and told me, "I really hope you are stopping at Swig & Swine. They are the best in Charleston, in my opinion." With all the world-class barbecue in Charleston, that was a bold statement to make. On short notice, I revised my travel plans and headed to Swig & Swine.

A native of Mantua, New Jersey, Anthony DiBernardo has had a lifelong passion for cooking. His first taste of cooking came when he was fourteen, when he began working as a banquet cook. A proud veteran, Anthony later served in the US Navy. It was that service to his country that brought Anthony to the Charleston area. Anthony started his own barbecue catering business, which ignited his passion. With a deep-rooted love for barbecue, coupled with a tenured culinary background, DiBernardo created the unique dining experience of Swig & Swine—a chef-driven barbecue concept using only wood as the fuel for the fire. Swig & Swine has become a fast favorite among enthusiasts worldwide. If you need proof, just check out the pins in the map at the restaurant, which shows customers visiting from all over the globe. As much as Anthony enjoys talking about barbecue, he is equally as spirited when he gets to talk about how the barbecue community comes together to support numerous local charities and educational programs.

The history of the Swig & Swine's location is almost as interesting as the restaurant's daily specials. The building was a former car wash on a main highway landscaped with strip malls and was revitalized and repurposed into a local barbecue joint. It's a beautifully laid out restaurant with a smoker in front and one out back. The bar area was alive with activity as the college football season had just kicked off. With a packed restaurant, you might expect a drop-off of service and product, but that was not the case at Swig & Swine. The pork belly sandwich, sausage, mac 'n' cheese and Brunswick stew were all on point. Save some room for dessert—the banana pudding and peanut butter pie are both worth the calories. Remember, if it tastes good it must be good for you.

SMOKED PORK BELLY

The pork belly at Swig & Swine is so succulent and savory I had to ask Anthony for the recipe. He said, "That is probably the easiest recipe we have." Ironically, I have found pork belly to be one item that is consistently made incorrectly. A simple salt and pepper rub and a strict adherence to time and temperature is essential for this cut of pork.

COOK TIME: 60 minutes   **YIELD:** 8 servings

1 (3-lb [1.4-kg]) skin-off pork belly
½ cup (144 g) kosher salt
½ cup (55 g) freshly ground black pepper

Rub the pork belly generously on both sides with the salt and pepper.

Prepare an indirect-heat smoker at 225°F (107°C). Place the pork belly fat side down and cook until the internal temperature reaches between 190 and 200°F (88 and 93°C), approximately 60 minutes. Wrap the pork belly in butcher paper and let it rest in a cooler for 1 hour.

BRUNSWICK STEW

Brunswick stew is a traditional fall stew in the southern United States. It was considered survival cuisine, or hunters' stew, among early settlers in the southern Appalachians. Fresh game and any local ingredients they had on hand were adapted to use in this stew. Typically, this is a thick tomato-based stew containing vegetables such as potatoes, tomatoes, lima beans, corn and okra. The meat is also a varied selection. Authentic Brunswick stew claims to use game meat such squirrel, opossum or rabbit, though today chicken or pork are the meats of choice. The stew simmers to allow the tougher meats to tenderize.

COOK TIME: 45 minutes   **YIELD:** 4 servings

½ large yellow onion, diced

1 large bell pepper, any color, diced

2 tsp (6 g) finely chopped garlic

Corn kernels from 2 medium ears corn

1 cup (75 g) blanched lima beans

1¼ cups (30 g) dry rub

1 cup (240 ml) chicken stock

1 cup (240 ml) sweet red-style barbecue sauce

1 lb (450 g) pulled smoked pork butt

In a large pot over medium heat, combine the onion, bell pepper, garlic, corn kernels and lima beans. Cook until the vegetables are tender, 8 to 10 minutes. Add the dry rub and toast the spices for 5 minutes. Add the chicken stock. Add the barbecue sauce and pulled pork and bring the stew to a simmer. Simmer for 30 to 40 minutes, until the flavors are combined.

THE SMOKE SHOP

SOMERVILLE, MASSACHUSETTS » ANDY HUSBANDS

325 Assembly Row
Somerville, MA 02145
www.thesmokeshopbbq.com

While the Northeast might not be synonymous with traditional barbecue, award-winning pitmaster and author Andy Husbands is defying that stereotype with his classic southern renditions in the Boston area. His work has not gone unnoticed, as *The Improper Bostonian* and *Boston* magazine have both awarded The Smoke Shop with top honors for 2018. The third location of Andy's popular barbecue joints is located in Assembly Row in Somerville, Massachusetts.

The Smoke Shop at Assembly Row is what might be called the sexiest barbecue joint on my journey. Long wooden communal tables in front of a massive facade of glass greet you as you walk up. It is stunning and only increases the anticipation of opening the large brown doors with their meat-cleaver handles. A clean, crisp, inviting space with much natural light, it is a food blogger's dream for photos. There was no doubt in my mind that the food was going to be insanely good for two reasons: First, Husbands has authored five cookbooks, been honored by the National Pork Board and his competition team won the Jack Daniels World Championship Invitational Barbecue. Second, I have competed against Andy in the past and have seen his team receive a bevy of award calls, so I know his food is great.

I started my trip to a food coma by ordering some pork belly with pickled peaches and some of The Smoke Shop's famous hot wings. The wings had a brown butter and habanero sauce that gives them the perfect balance of sweetness and heat. Next was a family-style serving of ribs, brisket, hot links, cornbread, bacon collards, zucchini salad and a hot catfish sandwich (because why not?). My table was covered with food; I contemplated holding my drink to make room for the next wave of plates. With locations in Cambridge, Boston and Somerville, the ability to get great Smoke Shop barbecue is never too far away.

BUTTER CAKE

My barbecue teammate and über-talented photographer, Ken Goodman, brought this recipe to fellow pitmaster Chris Hart and I to use in competitions. Also known as St. Louis ooey gooey cake, it's the perfect dessert: cakey, creamy and sugary. We won many first-place awards with this recipe, and so will you.

COOK TIME: 30 minutes   **YIELD:** 10 to 12 servings

¼ cup (48 g) granulated sugar

8 tbsp (120 g) butter, at room temperature

4 large eggs, divided

1 (16-oz [450-g]) box pound cake mix

16 oz (450 g) powdered sugar

8 oz (225 g) cream cheese, at room temperature

Preheat the oven to 350°F (177°C).

Grease a 9 x 13–inch (23 x 33–cm) cake pan, then dust it with the granulated sugar so all areas are coated. Tap out and discard any loose sugar.

In the bowl of a stand mixer, beat the butter, 2 of the eggs and the cake mix on low until combined. Transfer the batter to the prepared cake pan and smooth it with a spatula.

In another stand mixer bowl, beat the powdered sugar, cream cheese and the remaining 2 eggs on low until smooth. Spread this mixture over the cake batter.

Bake the cake for 30 minutes, or until the top is golden and pillowy and a toothpick inserted into the center comes out almost clean.

Transfer the cake to a rack to cool.

With a sharp knife, cut a ½-inch (13-mm) perimeter from around the edge of the cake. Cut the cake within that perimeter into 12 equal squares. Remove the crusty perimeter and save it for snacking. Place the squares on a serving platter and serve immediately, or cover the platter and refrigerate for up to 5 days.

PIG BEACH

BROOKLYN, NEW YORK » JEFF MICHNER AND MATT ABDOO

480 Union St.
Brooklyn, NY 11231
www.pigbeachnyc.com

Like a rack of his savory, unforgettable baby back ribs, Jeff Michner's childhood was basted with happy memories of tasting his grandma Bubba's cooking. Little did he know that as he attentively observed his Bubba work her culinary magic, Michner was silently building the foundation for a love of cooking that would last a lifetime.

In 2015, Michner was named executive chef at the new Pig Beach in Gowanus, Brooklyn, when it was a small seasonal pop-up. It was during this time that the Pig Beach name quickly gained accolades and numerous awards. Pig Beach officially opened as a permanent Brooklyn establishment in 2016, with Michner continuing to serve as the executive chef. With Michner at the helm, Pig Beach continued to gain success and accolades in NYC and became a staple for the Brooklyn community and a hot spot for many others.

Pig Beach has one of the most impressive layouts in the entire United States. The restaurant boasts an enormous outdoor section that is great for hanging out with a large group and also invites complete strangers to strike up conversations with one another. It's a venue big enough that they have hosted a guest pitmaster takeover series that saw some of the biggest names in barbecue come to New York, including Mike Mills, Carey Bringle and Pat Martin. Pig Beach is a pitmaster's dream—each corner of the outdoor space seems to have a smoker in it. With two large indoor communal spaces and bars, Pig Beach makes sure people have a place to go during the winter months.

Sadly, Chef Jeff Michner passed away in May 2018 at the age of thirty-six, leaving behind his wife, Sara, and daughter, Hayes. His culinary talents, kindness, contagious laugh and huge smile inspired everyone who knew him. Michner was highly respected and loved by his family, team and colleagues, and he quickly won over anyone he encountered. He will forever be remembered, and the legacy of who he was and what he built at Pig Beach will remain strong in our hearts.

LAMB BARBACOA

Traditionally, *barbacoa* is a preparation of meat (usually lamb, goat or beef) that is steamed in an underground oven until it is very tender and succulent. Today the term is also sometimes used for a similar preparation made in a smoker. The lamb barbacoa is a recipe of pure love, according to Matt Abdoo. It is like no lamb you have had before. It is meant to be shared with others.

COOK TIME: 5 to 6 hours   **YIELD:** 8 servings

DRY RUB

2 tbsp (36 g) kosher salt

1 tbsp (9 g) ancho chile powder

1 tbsp (9) guajillo chile powder

1 tbsp (9 g) ground cumin

2 tsp (2 g) dried oregano (preferably Mexican)

2 tsp (6 g) onion powder

2 tsp (6 g) garlic powder

1 tsp chipotle chile powder

¼ tsp ground cloves

To make the dry rub, mix together the salt, ancho chile powder, guajillo chile powder, cumin, oregano, onion powder, garlic powder, chipotle chile powder and cloves in a small bowl.

Prepare the smoker to cook indirectly at 250°F (121°C).

LAMB

1 (5-lb [2.3-kg]) boneless lamb shoulder roast, tied

1 ancho chile, stem and seeds removed

2 guajillo chiles, stems and seeds removed

4 cups (960 ml) chicken stock, divided

3 tbsp (45 ml) vegetable oil

½ cup (75 g) finely chopped white onion

4 cloves garlic, peeled and smashed

1 tsp dried oregano (preferably Mexican)

1 tsp ground cumin

¼ tsp ground cloves

¼ tsp ground cinnamon

⅓ cup (80 ml) apple cider vinegar

3 tbsp (32 g) finely chopped chipotles in adobo plus 1 tbsp (15 ml) adobo sauce

2 dried bay leaves

¼ cup (60 ml) fresh lime juice

Salt, to taste

To make the lamb, season the lamb shoulder roast liberally all over with the dry rub. Place the lamb in the smoker and smoke for 3 hours.

While the lamb is in the smoker, heat a large Dutch oven over medium heat. Add the ancho chile and guajillo chiles and toast them for 3 minutes until they are fragrant, turning them with tongs occasionally. Transfer the chiles to a small pot and cover them with 2 cups (480 ml) of the chicken stock. Bring the chicken stock to a boil over high heat, then reduce the heat to medium-low and cook until the chiles are completely softened, about 15 minutes. Set the pot aside.

In the now empty Dutch oven, heat the oil over high heat until it is shimmering. Add the onion and garlic and cook until they are browned, about 10 minutes. Add the oregano, cumin, cloves and cinnamon and cook until the spices are fragrant, about 30 seconds. Add the remaining 2 cups (480 ml) of chicken stock, vinegar and chipotles and bring the mixture to a boil. Reduce the heat to medium and simmer until the liquid is reduced by half, about 20 minutes.

Transfer the entire contents of the Dutch oven to a blender, along with the soaked chiles and their soaking liquid. Puree the ingredients until they are completely smooth, about 1 minute. Set the sauce aside.

Transfer the lamb to the now empty Dutch oven. Pour the sauce over the lamb and add the bay leaves. Place a lid on the Dutch oven slightly ajar, then transfer it to the smoker or a 250°F (121°C) oven. Cook until a metal skewer can be inserted into the lamb with little to no resistance, about 2 to 3 hours.

Transfer the lamb to a plate and discard the bay leaves. Place the Dutch oven on the stove and cook the sauce over medium-high heat until it is reduced by half, about 5 minutes, skimming any excess fat from the surface. Stir the lime juice into the sauce. Untie the lamb roast. The meat can be pulled and returned to the sauce if being served immediately; however, for the best flavor and most tenderness, place the lamb in a large bowl and cover it with the reduced sauce. Refrigerate the lamb and sauce overnight or up to 5 days. When you are ready to serve, remove the lamb from the liquid and pull it into large chunks with your hands or two forks. Place the sauce and shredded lamb into the Dutch oven and bring the mixture to a simmer over medium heat. Gently stir the lamb until it is warmed all the way through and thoroughly coated with the sauce. Season with salt to taste.

MICHNER'S DOWN SOUTH STEW

Jeff's take on the traditional Southern stew includes the well-balanced combination of brisket and chicken. I'm happy that Chef Michner's dream and passion can be shared with others.

COOK TIME: 2½ hours   **YIELD:** 8 servings

2 tbsp (30 ml) olive oil

2 cloves garlic, minced

1 small onion, diced

4 cups (960 ml) beef stock

¾ cup (180 ml) whole milk

½ cup (120 ml) Pig Beach Rob's Righteous Red BBQ Sauce

1 cup (240 ml) chili sauce

2 tsp (6 g) dark brown sugar

2 tsp (10 ml) Worcestershire sauce

1 tsp Hatch chile powder

½ tsp freshly ground black pepper

1 (14.5-oz [435-g]) can fire-roasted tomatoes, drained

1 cup (144 g) fresh corn kernels

1 cup (75 g) frozen lima beans

8 oz (240 g) cooked chicken thigh meat, coarsely chopped

8 oz smoked brisket, coarsely chopped

1 tsp salt

Fresh lemon juice, to taste

Hot sauce, for serving

Grilled bread, for serving

Heat the oil in a large Dutch oven over medium heat. Add the garlic and cook for 3 minutes, until it is aromatic and light golden brown. Add the onion and cook for 3 minutes, until it is soft and translucent.

Whisk in the beef stock, milk, Pig Beach Rob's Righteous Red BBQ Sauce, chili sauce, brown sugar, Worcestershire sauce, Hatch chile powder and pepper. Bring the mixture to a simmer then add the fire-roasted tomatoes, corn, lima beans, chicken and brisket.

Bring the stew to a simmer then reduce the heat to low and cover the Dutch oven. Cook for 2 hours. Season the stew with the salt and lemon juice.

Serve the stew with hot sauce and grilled bread.

BLACK'S BBQ

LOCKHART, TEXAS » KENT BLACK

215 N. Main St.
Lockhart, TX 78644
www.blacksbbq.com

The Black family started their barbecue joint back in 1932. Their claim is that Black's is the oldest barbecue restaurant run by one family in Texas. Third-generation pitmaster Kent Black and his son Barrett are running the show these days. The delicious meats they are so famous for are smoked in the original pit made by Edgar Black Jr. himself in 1949. This pit holds up to 500 pounds (225 kg) of meat!

Black's is not far from the downtown square. The traditional barbecue exterior matches the interior, where red-checkered tablecloths, wood paneling and taxidermy abound. But it's not the decor that draws the crowds to line up outside in the Texas heat—it's the food. Once you pick out your sides, it is time to get to the meat counter.

You're in Lockhart, Texas, so yes, the brisket is going to be out of this world. However, at Black's the rest of the menu is no slouch either. Enormous beef short ribs have as much as a 9-inch (23-cm) bone and weigh 1½ pounds (675 g). These ribs are a rich, moist hunk of beef that comes apart effortlessly. The flavor of Black's sausage is phenomenal, and their signature original sausage is the same recipe they served eighty-plus years ago. The jalapeño cheddar is just as excellent.

If you're lucky enough to be in the Lockhart area, Kent invites you down for lunch or dinner. "Bring your friends, family or coworkers for the best Lockhart barbecue you can find," he says.

GIANT BEEF RIBS

They say things are done bigger in Texas. They must have been enjoying a beef rib from Black's BBQ when they said that. These full-plate beef ribs are large enough to share with multiple people (or enjoy by yourself).

COOK TIME: 3½ to 5 hours   **YIELD:** 3 full-rib servings or 6 half-rib servings

3¾ cups (900 g) salt

¾ cup (83 g) freshly ground black pepper

3-bone beef ribs (full plate beef rib)

In a medium bowl, mix the salt and pepper together to make a rub. Place the rub in an airtight container. Sprinkle the rub on the top, bottom and sides of the beef ribs. Cover the ribs evenly with the rub and lightly rub the mixture into the meat.

Prepare the smoker to cook at 275°F (135°C) using a hardwood (oak is recommended).

Place the ribs in the smoker, meat side up, and cook 3½ to 5 hours, depending on the size of the rack, until the meat reaches an internal temperature of 195 to 205°F (91 to 96°C). The ribs are done when a probe or toothpick stuck between the bones (not on top of the bones) penetrates easily through the rack.

Let the meat rest for at least 15 to 20 minutes. Do not cut the individual ribs until you are ready to serve.

CREAMED CORN

Originating in Native American cuisine, creamed corn is now most commonly eaten in the midwestern and southern United States. It is an almost soupy version of sweet corn—but unlike other preparations of sweet corn, creamed corn is partially pureed, releasing the liquid of the kernels.

COOK TIME: 20 minutes   **YIELD:** 30 servings

8 cups (1.9 L) water

20 oz (600 g) sugar

¼ cup (38 g) minced garlic in oil

¼ cup (60 ml) pureed onion

2 tbsp (30 g) butter

1 (8-oz [240-g]) package cream cheese

7½ lb (3.4 kg) frozen corn

½ cup (120 ml) milk

8 oz (240 ml) cornstarch

2 tbsp (6 g) dried tarragon

In a large pot over medium-high heat, combine the water, sugar, garlic, onion, butter and cream cheese. Bring the mixture to a boil and stir. Add the corn and bring the mixture back to a boil.

In a medium bowl, combine the milk and cornstarch and add the mixture gradually to the pot, stirring constantly to avoid lumps. Let the creamed corn boil for 2 to 3 minutes, stirring constantly, then remove the pot from the heat. Add the tarragon and serve.

LEARN YOUR COOKERS

The type of cooker has almost no importance if you aren't familiar with your equipment. You could be cooking on a $5,000 smoker and if you aren't accustomed to it, you might just find yourself extinguishing dinner.

The cooker you choose will depend on how much product you want to smoke and what you're comfortable with. A little more of the technical inner workings of each is detailed in the following paragraphs.

BULLET SMOKERS

Bullet-style smokers are the most common and readily available from your local home improvement or barbecue store. These wood- and charcoal-fueled smokers can be used to cook directly or indirectly. Due to their oval shape and vent design, you can achieve a great smoke flavor because of the movement of air throughout. The Weber Smokey Mountain Cooker is the most popular bullet smoker. It's a product that can be used at home and in competition.

CERAMIC SMOKERS

Ceramic cookers, such as the Monolith BBQ Guru and Primo Oval XL 400, offer more cooking volume but are small enough to keep tucked away in the backyard. These *kamado*-style smokers have become popular with homeowners due to their versatility. Because of the ceramic construction, they are very fuel-efficient; however, they are also very heavy.

GRAVITY-FED SMOKERS

The term "gravity-fed" refers to how the fire is fed in the cooker. As the fire burns at the bottom, gravity continues to drop more charcoal down and feed the fire. Gravity-fed smokers are typically insulated and maintain consistent temperature throughout the cooking space. They typically have a larger cooking area and are fuel-efficient. For these reasons, gravity-feds are more expensive; however, the yield and consistency of this type of smoker make it a reasonable investment. My favorite gravity-fed smoker manufacturer is Deep South Smokers. Randal Bowman and his team create some of the best smokers I have ever seen or used.

OFFSET SMOKERS

The basic design of an offset smoker is a dual-chamber cooker, one to place the meat in and the other consisting of a firebox for wood or charcoal. These smokers use indirect heat only to cook and require traditional barbecue cooking techniques. Offset smokers are larger in size and offer an ample amount of options, from stainless steel sliding racks to reverse-flow cooking. Lang BBQ Smokers makes backyard, competition and light catering models. Those looking for a more serious commercial application can find their needs met at Mill Scale Metalworks.

PELLET SMOKERS

These come in a variety of sizes and run on wood pellets. These smokers are easy to use, light up quickly and maintain your desired temperature. They require electricity to keep the hopper feeding the firebox. My recommendation for the homeowner is Traeger grills. For those looking for a larger-volume pellet smoker with an insulated cabinet, I highly recommend the Fast Eddy's™ line by Cookshack.

HARDCORE CARNIVORE

AUSTIN, TEXAS » JESS PRYLES

www.jesspryles.com

www.hardcorecarnivore.com

Jess Pryles, creator of Hardcore Carnivore, is a cook, author and TV personality specializing in everything meat (namely beef). Jess has spent years educating herself in every aspect of the field, from education courses at Texas A&M University to hands-on training at ranches, butcher shops and slaughterhouses. Born and raised in Australia, Jess developed an appreciation and passion for Texas low-and-slow barbecue. She now resides in Austin, Texas, where she still oversees the Australasian Barbecue Alliance, a barbecue society that she cofounded to promote low-and-slow barbecue in Australia and New Zealand. Jess has been featured in numerous magazines and on television, including the Food Network and the *Today* show, among others. She is the creator of a line of unique meat seasonings called Hardcore Carnivore, and she has written a cookbook and designed her own signature edition offset smoker with the folks at Pitts & Spitts.

TEXAS SMOKED TRI-TIP STEAK

Jess recommends using oak when smoking tri-tip, although you could mix in some pecan, hickory or mesquite for a punchier flavor. She states the real trick to this dish is using the Hardcore Carnivore Black Steak and Meat Seasoning Rub—the short cooking time would not ordinarily give the meat enough time to develop a deep mahogany color on the outside, but her rub gives the appearance of bark that we usually expect from a six-hour cook.

COOK TIME: 45 minutes   **YIELD:** 4 to 6 servings

1 cup (240 ml) water

½ cup (120 ml) cider vinegar

1 (2- to 3-lb [900-g to 1.4-kg]) tri-tip steak

3 tbsp (27 g) Hardcore Carnivore Black Steak and Meat Seasoning Rub

Prepare the smoker to cook indirectly at 275°F (135°C).

Combine the water and vinegar in a half-size foil steam table water pan. Trim the tri-tip of any silver skin, sinew and excess surface fat. Dust the tri-tip with the Hardcore Carnivore Black Steak and Meat Seasoning Rub, ensuring all surfaces of the meat are well coated with the seasoning. Place the tri-tip in the smoker with the water pan underneath, and cook for 45 minutes, until the tri-tip reaches an internal temperature of 138°F (59°C). Remove the tri-tip and wrap it tightly in a double layer of foil, then place it in a warm cooler and let it rest for 45 minutes (see Tip). Once the tri-tip has rested, you can slice it against the grain to serve. The grain in tri-tip changes direction midway through the cut, so be prepared to switch directions.

TIP: *When the directions mention a warm cooler, note that the cooler doesn't need to be prewarmed—but it shouldn't be chilled or have recently held ice. Room temperature is fine.*

IZZY'S BROOKLYN SMOKEHOUSE

BROOKLYN, NEW YORK » SRULI "IZZY" EIDELMAN

397 Troy Ave.
Brooklyn, NY 11213
www.izzyssmokehouse.com

I kept hearing about Izzy's and knew I needed to experience it for myself. In 2017, they won the Brisket King of NYC competition. The panel of judges, which included Aaron Franklin, were blown away by the smoked brisket and pastrami, both of them kosher.

Izzy told me how he was always intrigued with barbecue—the more he researched it, the more he desired to make it. However, Izzy is devoutly Jewish. Keeping a kosher diet is a fact of life for him and his community. It would be a big challenge for him to gain acceptance into the world of barbecue. Imagine replicating barbecue flavors by just looking at it and smelling it.

The menu is concise and simple. (Sorry, no pork here—it's kosher, remember.) I enjoyed brisket, pastrami, brisket empanadas and some candied sweet potato. The tray is beautifully put together with pickled onions, pickles, cabbage and mustard. The brisket was very good—probably one of the best in NYC. But the pastrami! I could eat it every day, it was that good.

Izzy told me of the new location that he is working on and is hopeful to open soon. The location has an anticipated space of 5,000 square feet (465 sq m). I jokingly replied that I hoped I would have to wait an hour just to get in the door of the new place. For pastrami that good, I would wait all day.

SMOKED LAMB BREAST

Lamb isn't the most famous of barbecue meats, but it's fatty and slightly gamey, which means it's practically built for smoking. Lamb can be a little tricky to find in your local stores, but during the holidays most supermarkets will have a selection. If you can't find it, don't be afraid to ask your supermarket butcher to get some for you.

With lamb, you want to use a mild wood. Anything in the fruit family will work just fine, but be careful with harsher woods like hickory or oak. They can easily overpower the lamb and give it a foul taste. Remember, you want the lamb flavor to be the star, not the wood.

COOK TIME: 4 to 6 hours   **YIELD:** 6 servings

1 (3-lb [1.4-kg]) lamb breast

4 tbsp (72 g) plus 1 tsp kosher salt, divided

4 tbsp (24 g) plus ½ tsp freshly ground black pepper, divided

1 cup (240 ml) red wine vinegar

½ tsp finely chopped fresh rosemary

½ tsp finely chopped fresh thyme

2 cloves garlic, minced

½ cup (120 ml) vegetable oil

1 large white onion, thinly sliced and caramelized

Prepare the smoker to cook indirectly at 250°F (121°C). In a small bowl, combine 4 tablespoons (72 g) of the kosher salt and 4 tablespoons (24 g) of the pepper to make a rub. Apply a light layer of the rub to all sides of the lamb breast.

To create a baste, combine the vinegar, remaining 1 teaspoon salt, remaining ½ teaspoon pepper, rosemary, thyme and garlic in a medium bowl. Whisk in the oil.

Smoke the lamb for 4 to 6 hours (preferably over oak and cherrywood), basting it after the first hour and any time it looks dry, about every hour. The lamb breast is done when it reaches an internal temperature of 195 to 200°F (91 to 93°C).

Let the lamb breast rest for 15 minutes, then slice and serve it with the caramelized onion.

HOG HEAVEN

NASHVILLE, TENNESSEE » KATY GARNER

115 27th Ave. N.
Nashville, TN 37203
www.hogheavenbbq.com

Hog Heaven was established in 1986; there were three previous owners before Katy Garner and her husband, Andy, took it over in 1989. As if going into business wasn't stressful enough, Katy was pregnant at the time. Two weeks after giving birth, Katy was back behind the service window taking care of customers with her newborn son in a makeshift crib on the counter. It's that passion for her craft and desire to serve her community that you can taste in each bite at Hog Heaven.

Hog Heaven is located next to Centennial Park in Nashville, Tennessee. Their pork is smoked for more than fourteen hours and pulled by hand each morning. The word around Nashville was that I needed to try the chicken or turkey sandwich with Katy's "Kickin' Chicken" white barbecue sauce. When I arrived, the Hog Heaven crew was feverishly putting together a large catering order. Beyoncé and Jay-Z were in town and had just ordered wings and 5 gallons (19 L) of white sauce. The mayonnaise- and buttermilk-based sauce lived up to the hype with a savory, zesty flavor profile that enhanced the perfectly smoked chicken and turkey.

As I enjoyed my lunch, Katy brought over a warm peach cobbler and informed me that she wanted to share her recipe with us, a recipe that was given to her by her mother-in-law when they first started in 1989. It was delicious—sweet, juicy peaches baked with a buttery, cakey topping and all the sweetness you'd expect from a mother's recipe

Hog Heaven has also been featured on Food Network, Travel Channel and *Steve Harvey*. Not that Hog Heaven needed any more popularity, as the line for lunch from the local community can be in excess of sixty minutes. The outdoor seating and takeout-style restaurant lets you enjoy the beauty of the park and smell of the hickory wood burning on the Southern Pride out back.

PEACH COBBLER

A cobbler is a dish consisting of a fruit or savory filling poured into a large baking dish and covered with a batter, biscuit dough or dumpling dough before being baked. Some cobbler recipes, especially in the American south, resemble a thick-crusted, deep-dish pie with both a top and bottom crust. A cobbler should never be confused with a crumble.

COOK TIME: 45 minutes   **YIELD:** 8 servings

1½ lb (675 g) frozen peaches

2¾ cups (528 g) sugar, divided

2 cups (250 g) unbleached all-purpose flour

2 tsp (8 g) baking powder

½ tsp salt

8 tbsp (120 g) unsalted butter, divided

1 cup (240 ml) milk

Preheat the oven or barbecue to 350°F (177°C). Butter a 9 x 9–inch (23 x 23–cm) baking pan.

Place the peaches in a large bowl and top them with ¼ cup (48 g) of the sugar. Cover the bowl and let the peaches thaw so that the sugar creates a syrup.

In another large bowl, mix together the flour, 2 cups (384 g) of the sugar, baking powder and salt.

Melt 4 tablespoons (60 g) of the butter. Add the milk and the melted butter to the flour mixture. Stir until the batter is smooth and add it to the baking pan.

Top the batter with the peaches. Once the fruit is evenly distributed, distribute the remaining ½ cup (96 g) of sugar over the fruit and dot it lightly with the remaining 4 tablespoons (60 g) of butter.

Cook the cobbler for 45 minutes, or until it is brown and firm in the center. Serve warm.

I QUE

HOPKINTON, MASSACHUSETTS » CHRIS HART

Twitter @WickedGoodBBQ

When it comes to New England cuisine, most people think of dishes like lobster, clams and oysters as the trademarks of the area—not barbecue. However, The I Que barbecue team has people dropping the lobster rolls and picking up the rib bones, proving that good barbecue doesn't come only from the South. The I Que team started in 1997 when software engineer and cookbook author Chris Hart and chef Andy Husbands were working together at East Coast Grill.

Over the past two decades, Chris, Andy and their I Que team have been crowned grand champion at more than thirty competitive barbecue events across the country. More impressive, they were the first team from north of the Mason-Dixon Line to take first place in an event at the American Royal World Series of Barbecue® and to win the title of grand champion at the Jack Daniels World Championship Invitational Barbecue. Chris and Andy have written four cookbooks together: *Pitmaster*, *Wicked Good Barbecue*, *Grill to Perfection* and *Wicked Good Burgers*. Chris also appeared on season 2 of Food Network's *Chopped Grill Masters* and he has cooked at the James Beard House in NYC.

GOCHUJANG PORK RIBS

For most, barbecue is an inherently local cuisine. Chris is constantly working on dishes that debunk that ideology by combining traditional items with a twist. In this recipe, he takes advantage of that latitude and blends classic southern rib cookery with fermented Korean chile paste, *gochujang*. The result is a crispy, toothsome dry-rub rib. An offset smoker, a ceramic grill fitted with a plate setter or offset-grilling style on a kettle would all be great equipment choices.

COOK TIME: 3 hours   **YIELD:** 1 rack (6 bones)

I QUE DRY RUB #4

¼ cup (30 g) paprika

2 tbsp (36 g) kosher salt

2 tbsp (18 g) garlic powder

1 tbsp (9 g) gochugaru

½ tbsp (5 g) MSG

½ tbsp (5 g) ground coriander

½ tbsp (5 g) ground cumin

½ tsp curry powder

RIBS

1 (2½- to 3-lb [1.1- to 1.4-kg]) rack meaty loin back pork ribs

1 tbsp (16 g) yellow mustard

2 tbsp (30 ml) gochujang or other spicy Asian-style chile sauce

⅓ cup plus 1 tbsp IQUE dry rub #4, divided

To make the I Que dry rub #4, combine the paprika, salt, garlic powder, gochugaru, MSG, coriander, cumin and curry powder in a medium bowl. Store the rub in an airtight container for up to 2 weeks.

To make the ribs, remove the membrane from the back of the ribs using a paper towel. Rinse the ribs with cold water and place them on a large baking sheet. Brush the ribs with the yellow mustard and then with the gochujang. Refrigerate the ribs while you prepare the smoker.

Prepare the smoker or grill to cook indirectly at 300°F (149°C).

Remove the ribs from the refrigerator and sprinkle them with ⅓ cup (40 g) of the I Que dry rub #4. Place the ribs on the smoker.

Rotate the ribs every 45 minutes to ensure even cooking. Test the ribs for doneness by pulling 2 bones apart. After about 3 hours, when the meat starts to easily pull from the bone, the ribs are done. The internal temperature should be 185 to 195°F (85 to 91°C).

Remove the ribs from the smoker and sprinkle them with 1 tablespoon (9 g) of the I Que dry rub #4. Slice the ribs and serve.

LEROY AND LEWIS BARBECUE

AUSTIN, TEXAS   »   EVAN LEROY

121 Pickle Rd.
Austin, TX 78704
www.leroyandlewis.com

Known for his innovative takes on Texas barbecue, chef and pitmaster Evan LeRoy incorporates elements of fine dining and from-scratch cooking into his menu, shining a new light on the traditional cuisine at LeRoy and Lewis Barbecue. With a trailered smoker and food truck, the former founding pitmaster at Freedman's is looking to earn a place as one of Austin's elite with his innovative and ambitious offerings. He has garnered experience in such fine-dining restaurants as Hudson's On the Bend, while still finding time to barbecue at Hill Country Barbecue in NYC. While Evan is tending to the back of the house, his partner, Sawyer Lewis, is able to tend to the operations of the small business, which includes sourcing enough local product to meet the ever-increasing demand.

In addition to being named one of Zagat's 30 Under 30 rising stars in Austin's culinary world in 2014, Evan won the Austin Cochon555 in 2017 and was fittingly named King of Porc. The awards he earned are a direct representation of his passion and are well deserved. Out of all my visits on this trip, I might have been most inspired by my stop to see Evan. His brisket is one of the best you will enjoy in Austin; however, it was his creativity with such items like mac 'n' cheese–stuffed quail and meltingly delicious smoked beef cheeks that left me speechless.

SMOKED CONFIT BEEF CHEEKS

Beef cheeks are easily one of my favorite cuts to smoke. When treated right, they are delicious, sticky, gooey, gelatinous nuggets of beef. Often used in braises, stews and the classic taco filling barbacoa, beef cheeks require a long cook over low heat. If you've ever enjoyed great beef cheeks, you will already be familiar with their signature stickiness, a result of a thick seam of collagen that runs through the middle of the cheek. When taken to a high internal temperature, this collagen breaks down, helping ensure moist meat and providing the stickiness that draws people to this cut. Evan shared with me this great beef cheek recipe to try at home. In addition, he provided a cucumber salad (page 142) to pair with the beef cheeks.

COOK TIME: 8 hours   **YIELD:** 12 servings

5 lb (2.3 kg) beef cheeks

½ cup (144 g) kosher salt

1 cup (110 g) coarsely ground black pepper

1 gallon (3.8 L) rendered beef fat, melted

Trim the beef cheeks into a large fist shape. Also trim it of any scraggly bits or excess fat.

Mix the salt and pepper together in a medium bowl. Season the trimmed cheeks and scraps liberally with the mixture.

Prepare the smoker to cook indirectly at 250°F (121°C). Smoke the cheeks and scraps for about 4 hours with oak wood. Once a good crust has developed on the cheeks, drop them into a large pan of melted beef fat. Repeat this process with the scraps.

Put the pans of fat and cheeks back in the smoker for about 4 hours. The cheeks should be soft and tender but not falling apart. The scraps should be falling apart. Typically, the scraps take about an extra hour to get meltingly tender.

Strain the cheeks from the beef fat and let them cool to an internal temperature of 140°F (60°C). Strain the scraps and mix vigorously with tongs until the scraps are thoroughly combined.

Slice the cheeks and serve.

SAMBAL CUCUMBERS

Sambal is traditionally a spicy chile-based, all-purpose condiment found in many Asian and African countries. It's common in Southeast Asian countries like Malaysia and Indonesia, where it's more of a saucy paste in consistency. These sambal cucumbers work well with grilled meats, fish and chicken.

PREP TIME: 10 minutes   **YIELD:** 8 servings

3 large cucumbers
¼ cup (60 ml) sambal
1 cup (240 ml) rice vinegar
2 tsp (10 g) salt

Slice the cucumbers ⅛ inch (3 mm) thick on a mandoline. Place the cucumbers in a large bowl.

Combine the sambal and vinegar in a sealable container and shake to incorporate the two.

Toss the sambal mixture with the cucumbers. Season the cucumbers with salt.

LOVELESS CAFE

NASHVILLE, TENNESSEE » GEORGE HARVELL

8400 Hwy. 100
Nashville, TN 37221
www.lovelesscafe.com

In the 1950s, before the creation of the interstates we are accustomed to today, Highway 100 was the main thoroughfare to Nashville. Lon and Annie Loveless began serving fried chicken and biscuits to the hungry travelers. Soon their generosity turned into popularity and travelers would make the Loveless home a destination stop on their journey. Lon and Annie eventually converted their home into a restaurant and built a motel on the property for overnight guests.

Today, the Loveless Cafe's neon sign shines brightly as a symbol to travelers who are seeking a fine Southern meal. The motel has been revitalized over the years and now consists of a smokehouse, country market, gift shop and an event space for special occasions.

While the Loveless Cafe is world famous for their biscuits, it was their smokehouse that caught my attention. George Harvell has been the senior pitmaster at Loveless Cafe since 2003. From chicken to pork chops to turkey, George is in total control. However, it was a watermelon rib recipe he came up with that took best in show for me. George admits he wasn't sure what others' reactions would be, but he trusted the fact that the ribs tasted good to him. The sweetness of the watermelon is slightly pickled by the vinegar in the barbecue sauce. The ribs were paired with a side of creamed corn and turnip greens, which knocked the dish out of the park. This is a special dish and as a special it is served only on Thursday.

Miss Laura and Miss Wendy, Loveless Cafe's marketing and communications managers, exemplified the definition of Southern hospitality as they brought a giant bowl of banana pudding to the table. They said I had tried the biscuits, I had tried the ribs—it would be downright rude of me if I didn't try the dessert. I am not a person to burn a bridge and gladly grabbed a spoon. I am not sure if I had even finished my first bite before I started begging for the recipe. That banana pudding might have been the best dessert I had on my barbecue tour. The ladies were glad to give me the recipe, knowing it would put smiles on the faces of readers just like it did for me. Make sure you stop by Loveless Cafe on a Thursday and save some room for dessert.

WATERMELON RIBS

Ribs and watermelon are Southern staples—however, this might be the first time you ever see them together in the same recipe. When I think about this dish, the three words that come to mind are "tender," "flavorful" and "delicious." The sugar from the watermelon sweetens the ribs and the vinegar from the sauce all but pickles the watermelon for a balanced sweet and savory taste.

COOK TIME: 4 hours   **YIELD:** 4 (½-rack) servings

1 cup (120 g) Loveless Cafe Dry Rub

½ cup (72 g) brown sugar

2 (2½- to 3-lb [1.1- to 1.4-kg]) racks St. Louis ribs

2 cups (480 ml) Loveless Cafe Sweet with a Bite BBQ Sauce

3 cups (450 g) cubed watermelon

Prepare the smoker to cook indirectly for at 275°F (135°C).

In a small bowl, combine the Loveless Cafe Dry Rub and the brown sugar. Rub the ribs with the mixture, making sure to cover all the surfaces evenly.

Place the ribs in the smoker and cook for 2 hours, until the ribs reach an internal temperature of 145°F (63°C).

Remove the ribs from the smoker and cut them into 3-bone sections. Place the ribs in a medium roasting pan. Cover the ribs with the Loveless Cafe Sweet with a Bite BBQ Sauce and watermelon.

Wrap the pan tightly with foil. Increase the temperature of the smoker to 300°F (149°C) and cook for 2 hours, until the meat has reached an internal temperature of 190°F (88°C) and is falling off the bone.

Serve warm.

BANANA PUDDING WITH HOMEMADE WAFERS

This banana pudding recipe makes a classic Southern dessert. An heirloom family recipe, this homemade banana pudding should be an essential part of your holidays and celebrations!

COOK TIME: 40 minute   **YIELD:** 12 servings

PASTRY CREAM

1 cup (150 g) cornstarch

6 cups (1.4 L) whole milk, divided

18 large egg yolks

½ vanilla bean

2 cups plus 2 tbsp (408 g) sugar

To make the pastry cream, place the cornstarch in a large bowl. Add 2 cups (480 ml) of the milk to completely dissolve the cornstarch. Add the egg yolks to the mixture and whisk the ingredients together.

Split the vanilla bean open with a sharp knife and scrape the seeds out, reserving both the seeds and the pod. Place the vanilla seeds, vanilla pod and sugar in a large stainless steel pot. Add the remaining milk and bring the mixture to a boil over medium heat. Reduce the heat to low to prevent it from boiling over. With a small ladle, whisk a little of the hot milk mixture into the egg yolk mixture. Repeat this process until one-third of the hot milk mixture is whisked into the egg yolk mixture. Whisk this mixture into the remaining boiling milk and return it to a boil while you continue to whisk it. The mix will thicken quickly. Whisk for 1 minute.

Remove the pot from the heat and pour the pastry cream through a sieve into a large heatproof dish.

Place plastic wrap over the surface of the pastry cream to prevent a skin from forming and place it in the refrigerator to cool.

HOMEMADE WAFERS

2 cups (384 g) sugar, divided

6 large eggs

3⅓ cups (416 g) unbleached all-purpose flour

BANANA PUDDING

6 large ripe bananas, thinly sliced

2 cups (60 g) sweetened whipped cream

To make the homemade wafers, preheat the oven to 375°F (191°C).

Place 1¾ cups (336 g) of the sugar and eggs in the bowl of a stand mixer and mix on high speed for about 3 minutes, until it reaches the ribbon stage, just before soft peaks form (in the ribbon stage, the mixture will fall off the mixer's paddle in a ribbon when the paddle is lifted out of the mixture).

Sift the flour over the egg mixture in several batches, folding it in gently. Using a piping bag with a straight tip, pipe the batter into quarter-size wafers. Sprinkle liberally with the remaining ¼ cup (48 g) of sugar and bake the wafers for 10 to 12 minutes, until they are completely golden brown.

To make the banana pudding, spread a small amount of the pastry cream in the bottom of a trifle dish. Top the pastry cream with a layer of sliced bananas and then a layer of wafers. Spread enough pastry cream over the wafers to create a smooth, level surface. Repeat these steps to fill the dish, ending with a layer of pastry cream.

Cover the trifle dish well and allow the pudding to chill 6 to 8 hours in the refrigerator. Before serving, decorate with the whipped cream and additional wafers.

MAPLE BLOCK MEAT CO.

CULVER CITY, CALIFORNIA » DANIEL WEINSTOCK

3973 Sepulveda Blvd.
Culver City, CA 90230
www.mapleblockmeat.com

There is central-Texas brisket being served in Los Angeles. Pull into the parking lot and you're greeted with a wood stack, an offset smoker and the smell of peachwood in the air. You walk in, place your order with the cashier and make your way to the cutter, who will prepare your food.

While I waited for my brisket, turkey and sausage to be prepared, I noticed a couple J&R smokers in the back. "Am I in central Texas?" I wondered.

Mention brisket in a conversation with friends (or strangers) and one thing is certain: You will get an opinion—scratch that, you will get multiple opinions—on how to do it "right." There are many ways to smoke a whole brisket and hundreds of variations. However, there is no doubt that the team at Maple Block Meat Co. have developed their own process that works. To make a great brisket takes time, knowledge of your product and a love for great barbecue.

Maple Block's brisket is the best in California. Wood-smoked and covered in a simple yet effective salt and pepper rub, the meat is sliced to order and you can choose from fatty or lean cuts. I ordered the moist (i.e., fatty). Daniel Weinstock, the cofounder, managing partner and head pitmaster of Maple Block Meat Co., likes to keep the rub simple and states the most critical part of his brisket is the trimming—it's important to maintain the correct balance of fat cap to meat so it will render perfectly to produce the iconic bark that Maple Block Meat Co. is known for. The sausage and turkey both were excellent as well. Yet another homage to Texas, Maple Block Meat Co. keeps their turkey in a tray of melted butter at the cutting line.

Maple Block Meat Co. might be the most immaculate barbecue joint I've ever seen. A beautiful maple cutting area and meticulous open kitchen area and bar catch your eye when you walk in. The glass facade allows all that beautiful California sun to come beaming in. For those who prefer the open-air environment, there is a spacious outdoor patio as well.

If you're looking for the Texas trinity in La-La Land, you must stop at Maple Block Meat Co.

BRISKET

Briskets are the pectoral muscles from the chest of the steer, between the forelegs. There isn't much fat marbling within the muscle and there's a lot of connective tissue. That's why these muscles are so tough. There are two distinct muscles in a brisket: A long, flat, rectangular lean muscle that sometimes comes to a point that is called the flat, and a narrower, thicker, fattier, oval-shaped muscle called the point.

COOK TIME: 14 to 16 hours   **YIELD:** 20 servings

¾ cup (216 g) coarse salt

¼ cup (28 g) freshly ground black pepper

1 (14- to 16-lb [6.3- to 7.2-kg]) whole beef brisket

Combine the salt and pepper in a small bowl and transfer the mixture to a shaker.

Place the brisket on a large cutting board and carefully trim it with a sharp knife. After trimming the brisket, place the brisket on a large baking sheet and use the shaker to evenly distribute the rub over the entire brisket. Lightly massage the rub into the meat and set the brisket aside on the counter to come to room temperature, 1 to 2 hours.

Prepare the smoker to cook indirectly at a steady temperature of 225°F (107°C).

Place the brisket fat side up on the center rack of the smoker and cook for 14 to 16 hours. You do not need to check the meat during this time. Rather, keep the door or lid of the smoker closed and focus on maintaining a quality coal base and consistent heat.

After 14 hours, use a meat thermometer to check for an internal temperature of 185°F (85°C) in the thickest side of the brisket. Once that temperature is reached, open the door or lid of the smoker and allow the brisket to rest for 1 hour. This is a critical step because it allows the juices to settle and allows the temperature of the brisket to carry over to around 190°F (88°C).

Transfer the brisket to a large cutting board and slice it. The fully rested brisket will have a distinct bark with a light pink smoke ring under it and the inside will be tender and moist.

YOUR GO-TO SAUCES

The same way a fine wine can complement a dish, a good sauce can accent your barbecue. There are some purists out there who will declare that good barbecue doesn't need sauce—but for every yin, there is a yang. For me, it's more important that a sauce is used well more than whether a sauce is used at all. A sauce should be treated as a finishing tool. For example, apply sauce to your ribs and then return them to the smoker to let the sauce set. Cooking the ribs for just a few minutes to let the sugars in the sauce start to blend but not burn can make all the difference.

PIEDMONT CAROLINA SAUCE

Piedmont Carolina sauce is a thin vinegar-based sauce that is very tangy and served as a mop sauce and finishing sauce for pulled pork. It is even great as a mop sauce for smoked ribs.

COOK TIME: 20 minutes   **YIELD:** 2 cups (480 ml)

1 cup (240 ml) ketchup

1 cup (240 ml) water

¼ cup (60 ml) apple cider vinegar

1 large onion, finely chopped

3 cloves garlic, crushed

2 tbsp (18 g) brown sugar

2 tbsp (30 ml) molasses

In a medium pot over low heat, combine the ketchup, water, vinegar, onion, garlic, brown sugar and molasses. Bring to a simmer and cook for 20 minutes. Strain the sauce and serve.

HONEY MUSTARD BARBECUE SAUCE

This sweet honey mustard barbecue sauce works great on poultry, seafood and pork. Easy to make ahead or while you wait for the grill to come to temperature, you can store it for up to a week in your refrigerator.

PREP TIME: 30 minutes   **YIELD:** 1¾ cups (360 ml)

½ cup (120 ml) Dijon mustard

¼ cup (60 ml) apple cider vinegar

¼ cup (60 ml) ketchup

¼ cup (60 ml) molasses

¼ cup (60 ml) honey

¼ cup (60 ml) maple syrup

In a medium bowl, whisk together the mustard, vinegar, ketchup, molasses, honey and maple syrup until combined.

Cover the bowl and let the sauce sit for at least 30 minutes. This recipe can be made a couple days ahead of when you will need it.

BASIC BARBECUE SAUCE

The name says it all. This sauce is easy to whip up. It is sweet and thick and with a slight taste of onion. It's great on just about anything that comes off the barbecue. Feel free to get creative and make your own variation.

COOK TIME: 45 minutes   **YIELD:** 3 cups (720 ml)

3 tbsp (45 g) salted butter

1 large yellow onion, diced

2 tsp (6 g) minced garlic

2 cups (480 ml) ketchup

½ cup (120 ml) dark molasses

⅓ cup (80 ml) apple cider vinegar

⅓ cup (48 g) dark brown sugar

1 tbsp (9 g) chili powder

1 tsp cayenne pepper

1 tsp freshly ground black pepper

Melt the butter in a small pot over medium-high heat. Add the onion and garlic and cook until they have softened, about 3 minutes.

Add the ketchup, molasses, vinegar, brown sugar, chili powder, cayenne pepper and black pepper, stirring until fully combined. Bring the mixture to a boil then reduce the heat and simmer until the mixture has thickened, 30 to 40 minutes.

Remove the sauce from the heat and let it cool. Transfer the sauce to a blender and blend until smooth. Store the sauce in the refrigerator for up to 1 month.

301 Center Ave.
Westwood, NJ 07675
www.kimchismoke.com

In 2007, Robert Cho—born in Seoul, South Korea, and living in Hackensack, New Jersey—was working as a real estate broker. One day, watching a contestant on *Throwdown with Bobby Flay* smoke ribs over smoldering wood, he found his calling. After several years of private catering, competitions and pop-ups, Robert opened his restaurant Kimchi Smoke. In 2018, Robert once again was watching Bobby Flay on television—only this time it was the episode where he and Flay squared off on Food Network's *Beat Bobby Flay*.

The barbecue at Kimchi Smoke is crazy good. The best way to describe it is southern barbecue with a Korean flare. "I'm very big on my food not being called fusion," Robert says. "As a Korean-American, I am 100 percent Korean and 100 percent American. Eating my food, people realize it is American-style barbecue, which is defined by slow smoking, as opposed to grilling. The menu has elements of Korean cuisine, such as kimchi, but it is not fusion cooking." If Texas is the barometer of rating someone's brisket then Kimchi Smoke gets a big star. It's buttery, it's peppery and it's smoked.

The menu at Kimchi Smoke makes you think outside the box from your typical barbecue setting. If you go on a Friday or Saturday, you can try a Chonut, which consists of piled brisket, bacon, cheddar, smoked kimchi, chipotle sauce and scallions all served on a glazed doughnut. An interesting dish I was able to sample were the Korean Ribs. They were smoked with cherrywood and topped with a gochujang glaze and sesame seeds. It was difficult to put the correct adjective on this dish. *Sweet? Savory? Spicy?* Regardless, they were excellent. I also tried an Austin Cho sandwich: chopped brisket, chipotle sauce, kimchi and scallions on a roll. The food at Kimchi Smoke was so good I got back in line to get a pound of brisket and some ribs to take home.

KOREAN RIBS

It is exciting to watch the world of barbecue transition from the traditional flavor profiles to variations that embrace global tastes and preferences. Robert shares with us his deviation from the norm that includes gochujang and soy sauce.

COOK TIME: 5¼ hours   **YIELD:** 1 rack (10 to 12 bones)

KIMCHI SMOKE BBQ RUB

2 tbsp (18 g) paprika

2 tbsp (18 g) ground cumin

2 tbsp (18 g) garlic powder

2 tbsp (15 g) granulated onion

2 tbsp (18 g) ground gochugaru (Korean red pepper flakes)

1 tbsp (15 g) salt

1 tbsp (6 g) freshly ground black pepper

1 tbsp (9 g) ground ginger

KIMCHI SMOKE SAUCE

½ cup (120 ml) gochujang

¼ cup (60 ml) soy sauce

¼ cup (60 ml) mirin

2 tbsp (30 ml) sesame oil

1 tbsp (9 g) ground gochugaru

¼ cup (60 ml) honey

¼ cup (60 ml) water

RIB SPRAY

½ cup (120 ml) apple cider vinegar

½ cup (120 ml) water

RIBS

1 (3-lb [1.4-kg]) rack St. Louis–cut pork ribs

¼ cup (12 g) diced scallions

1 tbsp (6 g) sesame seeds

To make the Kimchi Smoke BBQ rub, combine the paprika, cumin, garlic powder, granulated onion, ground *gochugaru*, salt, pepper and ginger in a small bowl. Transfer the rub to a shaker.

To make the Kimchi Smoke sauce, combine the gochujang, soy sauce, mirin, oil, gochugaru, honey and water in a small bowl.

To make the rib spray, combine the vinegar and water in a food-safe spray bottle.

To make the ribs, pull back the ribs' membrane with a paper towel. Trim any excess fat and make the ribs a uniform rectangular shape. Lightly dust the ribs on both sides with ¼ cup (30 g) of the Kimchi Smoke BBQ rub. Dust only the meat on the back side of the ribs.

Prepare the smoker to cook indirectly at 250°F (121°C) using cherrywood.

Cook the ribs for 3 hours. Spray every hour, or every time you open the smoker, with the rib spray. After 3 hours, spray the ribs again and wrap them in foil. Cook for 1½ hours. Remove the ribs from the foil and place them back in the smoker, bone side down, and cook for 30 minutes.

Lightly brush the ribs with 2½ cups (600 ml) of the Kimchi Smoke sauce and put the ribs back in the smoker for 15 minutes to set the sauce. The ribs' internal temperature should be 185 to 195°F (85 to 91°C).

Remove the ribs from the smoker and let them rest for 15 minutes. Slice the ribs and garnish with the scallions and sesame seeds.

SMOKIN' HOGGZ BBQ

ABINGTON, MASSACHUSETTS » BILL GILLESPIE

www.smokinhoggzbbq.com

You probably don't think of Abington, Massachusetts, when thinking about great barbecue. However, pitmaster Bill Gillespie and the Smokin' Hoggz team are proving that good barbecue has no regional limitations. Bill spends his days working for the local utility company as a design engineer, but his true passion is grilling and cooking barbecue.

For more than twenty-five years, Bill has been perfecting his craft in barbecue, cooking in his backyard for friends and family. In 2005, Bill joined the barbecue circuit and in 2008 formed Smokin' Hoggz BBQ. Since then he has gone on to win multiple grand championships and numerous awards, including Northeastern Barbecue Society Team of the Year in 2014 and 2015, the 2011 Jack Daniels World Championship Invitational Barbecue and the 2014 American Royal World Series of Barbecue (the latter two being some of the most prestigious competitions on the circuit). In addition to being an elite pitmaster, Bill, has also authored three barbecue cookbooks: *Secrets to Smoking on the Weber Smokey Mountain Cooker and Other Smokers*, *The Smoking Bacon and Hog Cookbook* and *The Secrets to Great Charcoal Grilling on the Weber*.

COMPETITION ST. LOUIS PORK RIBS

Bill's eyes light up when he talks about ribs. Admittedly, they are the obsession that got him into competition BBQ. When cooked right, St. Louis ribs are juicy, tender and oh so flavorful. Here is the recipe that has helped Smokin' Hoggz win the Northeastern BBQ Society Ribs Team of the Year two years in a row!

COOK TIME: 4 to 4½ hours   **YIELD:** 8 (½-rack) servings

4 (2½- to 3-lb [1.1- to 1.4-kg]) racks St. Louis–cut spareribs

Twist'd Q Smokin' Hoggz Smokin' Applewood All-Purpose Rub

2 cups (480 ml) honey

2 cups (288 g) brown sugar

8 tbsp (120 g) butter

2½ cups (480 ml) Smokin' Hoggz Barbecue Sauce, divided

Prepare the barbecue for indirect cooking at 250 to 275°F (121 to 135°C) using about 4 hefty chunks of apple and maple wood. Note that the wood should be added just prior to putting the ribs on the barbecue.

With meat side facing down, apply the Smokin' Hoggz all-purpose rub to the back side of the ribs. Let the rub set up for about 10 minutes. Flip the ribs over and apply additional rub to the meat side. Let the rub set up for about 15 minutes, then apply another coating of rub to the meat side. Let the ribs sit for 30 minutes. Put the ribs, meat side up, in the barbecue and cook for 3 hours.

Lay out 4 large sheets of the heavy-duty foil. To each sheet, apply ¼ cup (60 ml) of honey, ¼ cup (48 g) of brown sugar and 2 tablespoons (30 g) of butter, then lay the ribs, meat-side down, on the foil. To the ribs, apply ¼ cup (60 ml) of honey, ¼ cup (48 g) of brown sugar and ½ cup (120 ml) of the Smokin' Hoggz Barbecue Sauce and wrap them in the foil tightly. Note that you may want to double-wrap your ribs to keep the ribs from tearing through the foil when putting them back on the barbecue.

Place the wrapped ribs in the barbecue and cook for 1 hour, then check the ribs for doneness. To check if the ribs are done, look at the back side of the ribs. The meat will have shrunk from the bone about ¼ to ½ inch (6 to 13 mm) and the bones will start to pop through on the back side. The internal temperature should be 185 to 195°F (85 to 91°C). If the ribs are done, remove them from the barbecue and open the foil to let them vent for about 10 minutes. This will stop them from cooking any further.

Take about ½ cup (120 ml) of the juices from the foil and the remaining ½ cup (120 ml) of Smokin' Hoggz Barbecue Sauce and combine them in a small bowl to use as a glaze. Glaze the ribs, cut them into individual portions and serve.

ARMADILLO EGGS

As you can imagine, there is some downtime as you're waiting for your ribs to cook. Bill tries to make the most of this time by creating recipes that his friends and family will enjoy. He had a fiendish smile when he offered up his recipe for a fun party snack he likes to call Armadillo Eggs.

COOK TIME: 1 to 1½ hours   **YIELD:** 24 Armadillo Eggs

8 oz (240 g) cream cheese, softened

1 cup (120 g) shredded cheddar cheese

2 cloves garlic, minced

Salt, as needed

6 large jalapeños, stems removed

1 lb (450 g) Jimmy Dean brand regular sausage

1 lb (450 g) ground Italian sausage

8 oz (240 g) ground chourico or chorizo sausage

24 strips bacon

All-purpose barbecue dry rub, as needed

1 cup (240 ml) ranch dressing

Prepare the barbecue to cook indirectly at 250°F (121°C). If you have a water pan, fill it about halfway with warm to hot water.

In a medium bowl, mix together the cream cheese, cheddar cheese and garlic until combined. Taste the mixture and add salt if needed.

Cut the jalapeños in half lengthwise. Scoop out the seeds and then cut the sliced jalapeños in half, so that 1 jalapeño yields 4 quarters. Place about 1 teaspoon of the cream cheese filling in each jalapeño quarter.

Combine the Jimmy Dean brand regular sausage, Italian sausage and chourico sausage in a small bowl. Form ⅓ cup (75 g) of the sausage into a 3-inch (7.5-cm) circle. Place a stuffed jalapeño in the center of the sausage. Wrap the sausage around the stuffed jalapeño until it's completely covered and form it into an egg shape. Wrap the egg with 1 bacon strip, making sure the seam is facing down. Season the egg with the dry rub. Repeat this process with the remaining sausage, jalapeño quarters and bacon strips.

Place the sausage-wrapped jalapeños directly on the top grate of the barbecue. Cook for 1 to 1½ hours, or until the sausage reaches an internal temperature of 165°F (74°C). Serve with the ranch dressing.

90 Kent Ave.
Brooklyn, NY 11249
www.monksmeats.com

Over the years, there are certain friendships and business relationships that you make. One I made and cherish is my relationship with Sean Ludwig, who is the man behind the social media handle NYCBBQ. If there is anyone who knows what is going on in the New York and New Jersey areas in regard to barbecue, it is him. When word got out about the project I was working on, Sean and I got together to discuss the state of barbecue. He told me that the landscape of New York City barbecue is changing and that I needed to get out to Smorgasburg in Brooklyn, that there was a barbecue purveyor by the name of Monk's Meats I needed to check out.

I soon discovered that Chris Kim, the owner of Monk's Meats, owns one of only three vegan barbecue joints in the United States and the only one in NYC. Chris has been a vegetarian since about 1996 and his interest in barbecue is a direct result of twenty years of being served dry portobello mushrooms and cardboard veggie burgers at friends' cookouts. He makes his meatless "meats" in-house. His primary "meat" is known as *seitan* and is made from wheat flour. It's cooked as part of its production process, so smoking is for flavor, texture and preservation. Chris draws inspiration from many regional American barbecue traditions and open-fire cooking worldwide.

When you visit Monk's Meats at Smorgasburg, you would have no idea that this barbecue vendor is vegan. The smell of smoke in the air and the line of people waiting suggested they were about to pull brisket or ribs off the pit. Instead, the crowd of faithful followers was being treated to a smoked jerk seitan sandwich with jicama slaw and roasted pineapple. They were also serving barbecue seitan sandwiches with slaw and pickles. Chris has the traditional low-and-slow method of cooking and steered barbecue in a brave new direction. His barbecue has great flavor and is well received by everyone in the vegan community. Keep up the great work, Chris.

HOT PULLED OYSTER MUSHROOMS

Chris was happy to share with me one of his favorite recipes—Hot Pulled Oyster Mushrooms. The easiest way to shred the mushrooms is a technique that most will be familiar with: using two forks. By using the forks to pull the mushrooms in opposite directions, you get a great shredded effect that resembles pulled pork.

COOK TIME: 1¼ hours **YIELD:** 6 servings

MUSHROOMS

1½ lb (675 g) oyster mushrooms

¾ cup (216 g) kosher salt

½ cup (72 g) brown sugar

½ cup (60 g) paprika

¼ cup (30 g) ground mustard

¼ cup (28 g) freshly ground black pepper

HOT SAUCE

2 cups (480 ml) apple cider vinegar

1 tbsp (9 g) brown sugar

1 tbsp (9 g) cayenne pepper

1 tsp salt

1 tsp freshly ground black pepper

Separate the leaves of the oyster mushrooms by pulling each from the main body. Shred the larger mushroom leaves intro strips by hand.

In a large bowl, combine the salt, brown sugar, paprika, mustard and black pepper. Toss the mushrooms with the rub.

Prepare the smoker to cook indirectly at 225°F (107°C), using apple or pecan wood.

Place the mushrooms in a half-size aluminum steam pan and smoke for approximately 1 hour. After about 45 minutes, the mushrooms should be soft and starting to break down.

In a medium pot over medium-high heat, combine the vinegar, brown sugar, cayenne pepper, salt and black pepper. Simmer until the sugar is completely dissolved. Deglaze the mushrooms with the hot sauce and return them to the smoker to allow the sauce to set up. After 15 minutes, remove the mushrooms from the smoker and serve.

ANCHO-SMOKED SEITAN

Although it is made from wheat, seitan has little in common with bread. Seitan becomes surprisingly similar to the look and texture of meat when cooked, making it a popular meat substitute. Seitan is high in protein and is a popular protein source for vegetarians and vegans: 1 ounce (30 g) of seitan provides 21 grams of protein. Seitan has a savory taste, probably closest to plain chicken or a portobello mushroom, but can take on many more flavors from different recipes.

COOK TIME: 2½ hours   **YIELD:** 6 servings

SEITAN

22 oz (660 g) vital wheat gluten

½ cup (30 g) nutritional yeast

1 tbsp (7 g) ground flaxseed

1 tbsp (9 g) onion powder

1 tbsp (9 g) garlic powder

1 tsp salt

6 cups (1.4 L) vegetable broth, divided

¼ cup (66 g) tomato paste

1¼ cups (300 ml) soy sauce, divided

2 tbsp (30 ml) molasses

To make the seitan, combine the vital wheat gluten, nutritional yeast, flaxseed, onion powder, garlic powder and salt in a large bowl. Mix well to distribute the ingredients evenly.

In another large bowl, combine 3 cups (720 ml) of the vegetable broth, tomato paste and ¼ cup (60 ml) of the soy sauce. Pour the broth mixture into the gluten mixture, reserving a small amount of the broth mixture. Quickly distribute the liquid through the gluten mixture and knead for 1 minute, until most of the dry mix is incorporated. Add the reserved broth mixture and knead until all of the gluten mixture is incorporated. Form the dough into a ball. Let the dough ball rest for 10 minutes.

In a large pot over high heat, combine the remaining 3 cups (720 ml) of vegetable broth, the remaining 1 cup (240 ml) of soy sauce and molasses. Cover the pot.

Using a sharp knife, cut the dough ball into 1½- to 2-inch (4- to 5-cm) thick slabs. Bring the broth mixture to a boil. Add the seitan slabs to the broth, fully submerging them. Boil for 5 minutes, until all the slabs start to float. Reduce the heat to low and simmer for 1 hour. For best results, let the seitan cool before using.

(continued)

ANCHO-SMOKED SEITAN (CONTINUED)

COFFEE RUB

1 (6 g) coarsely ground coffee

1 tbsp (18 g) kosher salt

2 tsp (6 g) light brown sugar

2 tsp (6 g) smoked paprika

2 tsp (6 g) chili powder

1 tsp garlic powder

1 tsp onion powder

1 tsp ground cumin

1 tbsp (6 g) freshly ground black pepper

ANCHO BUTTER

2 large ancho chiles

1 cup (240 ml) water

4 oz (120 g) vegan butter, softened

While the seitan is simmering, make the coffee rub. Combine the coffee, salt, brown sugar, smoked paprika, chili powder, garlic powder, onion powder, cumin and pepper in a large bowl. Mix until the ingredients are incorporated.

Score the surface of the cooled seitan slabs with a knife, being careful not to cut too deeply. Rub the exterior of the seitan slabs with the coffee rub, applying it generously all over the slabs. Cover the seitan slabs and let them rest overnight, or at least 1 hour, in the refrigerator.

When the seitan slabs are almost done resting, make the ancho butter. Soak the ancho chiles in the water for at least 1 hour.

Drain and reserve the soaking water. Transfer the chiles to a blender and process. Add the reserved water, 1 tablespoon (15 ml) at a time, until the anchos are blended into a thick paste. Reduce the blender speed to low and add the butter. Blend until the mixture is homogeneous.

Prepare the smoker to cook indirectly at 200°F (93°C), using hickory wood.

Place the seitan slabs on the grill rack on the cool side of the smoker and cook for 20 minutes. Flip the slabs over and baste them generously and evenly with the ancho butter on the side that is now facing up.

Every 15 minutes for 90 minutes, flip the seitan slabs and baste them generously with ancho butter.

Remove the seitan slabs from the smoker and let them rest for 10 minutes.

Thinly slice the seitan slabs and dress them with any remaining ancho butter or your favorite barbecue sauce.

LOCKHART SMOKEHOUSE

DALLAS, TEXAS » JILL BERGUS, JEFF BERGUS AND TIM MCLAUGHLIN

400 West Davis
Dallas, TX 75208
www.lockhartsmokehouse.com

Only a few can say they were born into a barbecue legacy. Jill Bergus is one of them. Her grandfather, Edgar "Papa" Schmidt, owned and ran the stellar Kreuz Market in Lockhart, Texas. The little town of Lockhart has been recognized as the barbecue capital of Texas. In 2011, Jill and her husband, Jeff, teamed up with pitmaster Tim McLaughlin to bring central-Texas barbecue to Dallas.

With more than a hundred years of barbecue history and reputation as their guides, Jill, Jeff and Tim are inspired to create the best barbecue they can. It was important for Jill to be able to share the high-caliber barbecue of Lockhart with the folks of Dallas. As you approach Lockhart Smokehouse, you begin to get the smell of the post oak smoke. As you would expect at a traditional barbecue joint, all specials are written on a board daily and crossed off when sold out. Also a famed Lockhart tradition: no plate, no forks and no sauce. Don't worry—be kind to the cashiers and they will give you a fork if you ask.

It takes one bite to realize that Lockhart Smokehouse is a central-Texas barbecue joint. As you would expect, the brisket is phenomenal. They also have shoulder clod on the menu, which is a leaner cut compared to brisket, but it is packed with beef flavor. And I would be remiss if I didn't mention the Kreuz sausages. Lockhart Smokehouse is the only place in the Dallas area where you can get the authentic 110-year-old recipe.

If you can't get to either their Dallas or Plano locations, fear not. Jill informed me that they have teamed up with Goldbelly to offer nationwide shipping of their products. Visit their website to order.

SMOKED LAMB CHOPS

There are three kinds of lamb that work on the barbecue: loin chops, shoulder chops and rib chops. I find loin chops work best. There is very little prep needed for loin chops—they are pretty much ready right out of the pack from your butcher, which makes them quick enough for a weeknight meal and elegant if entertaining. Lamb has a very rich taste (more so than beef) and also has a lot of fat, so you can expect the meat to be extra juicy when cooked properly—for me that's medium rare. These lamb chops are loaded with tenderness and flavor.

COOK TIME: 45 minutes   **YIELD:** 4 servings

3 tbsp (54 g) kosher salt

1 tbsp (6 g) freshly ground black pepper

1 tbsp (9 g) paprika

1 tbsp (9 g) onion powder

2 tbsp (18 g) brown sugar

4 (4-oz [120-g]) lamb loin chops

In a small bowl, combine the salt, pepper, paprika, onion powder and brown sugar. Season both sides of the lamb loin chops with the rub and let them rest for 30 minutes.

Prepare the barbecue to cook indirectly at 250°F (121°C), using post oak wood. Smoke the lamb for 45 minutes, or until its internal temperature reaches 145°F (63°C).

BLUE CHEESE COLESLAW

Anyone who's ever been to a barbecue joint or rib shack knows about red slaw: finely chopped cabbage with either a tangy apple cider vinegar or mayonnaise dressing, usually served atop a pork sandwich or in a soufflé cup. It's treated almost like a condiment. However, the slaw served at Lockhart's Smokehouse takes a back seat to no one. From the crunch of the cabbage to the heat of the jalapeño and tangy bite of the blue cheese, this is one savory dish that is a must for your next barbecue party.

YIELD: 10 servings

1 small head purple and green cabbage, thinly sliced

1½ cups (330 g) mayonnaise

2 tbsp (24 g) sugar

1 tbsp (15 ml) apple cider vinegar

Salt, to taste

Freshly ground black pepper, to taste

1 finely diced jalapeño, seeds removed (optional)

¼ cup (38 g) crumbled blue cheese

Place the cabbage in a large bowl. In a medium bowl, whisk together the mayonnaise, sugar, vinegar, salt and pepper. Pour the mayonnaise dressing over the cabbage and toss. Add the jalapeño, if using, and crumbled blue cheese and toss to combine them. Cover the bowl with plastic wrap and refrigerate for a few hours to allow the flavors to meld before serving.

Chef and pitmaster Mario Chape has been doing barbecue pop-ups since before anyone knew what a pop-up was. It wasn't until after a trip to Houston that Mario, a Johnson and Wales–trained chef, started his journey into barbecue. The son of a Cuban father and Puerto Rican mother, Big Papa had bold flavors and sweet spice in his DNA. Now it was up to him to figure out how to translate that into barbecue.

The first time I ate at Big Poppa's was at one of his acclaimed pop-ups in NYC. I stumbled across Mario by chance. Mario was holding court with those gathered around, sharing his knowledge and relating to folks on the street as only Mario can. That day he was featuring his version of a Cuban sandwich called the *que-ban*.

Regardless of whether it is one of his pop-ups, a catering event or festival, if there is a barbecue event in the NYC area, you will probably find Mario working. It is his love of barbecue and his fellow pitmasters that drives him to help whenever he can. He has cooked at the James Beard House with the Ubon's BBQ family, worked countless events for Food Network chef Carl Ruiz and volunteered his time and equipment to assist Operation BBQ Relief. If you ever visit the Big Apple Barbecue Block Party, you can probably see Mario jumping from tent to tent lending a hand. If you live in the New York or New Jersey metro area or plan to visit, I highly advise bookmarking Papa Smoke'M's Instagram to see where he is going to pop up next.

LECHON PORK SHOULDER

Lechon is a Spanish word referring to a roasted suckling pig. It is also the national dish of Puerto Rico. Mario applies those same techniques and process to a pork shoulder to provide us with an out-of-this-world recipe. It is flavorful, succulent and spicy—everything you would expect from an authentic dinner in Puerto Rico.

COOK TIME: 10 hours   **YIELD:** 12 servings

Freshly ground black pepper, as needed

Kosher salt, as needed

4 tbsp (36 g) ground cumin

3 tbsp (9 g) dried oregano

2 tbsp (30 ml) extra virgin olive oil

8 cloves garlic, peeled and gently smashed

¼ tsp red pepper flakes

1 cup (240 ml) fresh orange juice

1 cup (240 ml) fresh lime juice

1 cup (240 ml) low-sodium chicken broth

2 dried bay leaves

1 (8-lb [3.6-kg]) pork shoulder

Fresh lemon juice, for serving

1 medium Spanish onion, thickly sliced

Prepare the smoker to cook indirectly at 250°F (121°C).

In a food processor, combine the pepper, salt, cumin, oregano, oil, garlic and red pepper flakes and pulse. Slowly add the orange juice, lime juice, chicken broth and bay leaves and pulse until the mixture is smooth.

Thoroughly coat the pork butt with the rub mixture. Reserve any leftover rub mixture.

Place the pork butt in the smoker and cook for 4 hours. Remove the pork butt and place it in a half-size aluminum steam pan with the remainder of the rub mixture. Baste with the juices in the pan every 30 minutes through the next 6 hours of cooking.

When the pork has reached an internal temperature of 195°F (91°C) and is fork-tender, pull the meat and serve it with a splash of fresh lemon juice and raw Spanish onion. Reserve the leftover meat for the Cubano Sandwich (page 178).

CUBANO SANDWICH

It's a debate as old as time: Where do you go to get a Cubano sandwich? Who makes the most authentic one? Mario Chape answers both those questions with this classic and perfect recipe. Part of the charm of the Cubano sandwich comes from its simplicity. With no vegetables in sight and far better when slathered in butter, the magic between the spiced bread comes with a story of heritage, pedigree and authentic culture. In keeping with tradition, the best sandwich maintains its purity from the top of the first slice to the bottom of the second. There's a story behind each diagonally sliced bit of goodness, but the debate for where to find one will be no more.

COOK TIME: 15 minutes   **YIELD:** 1 serving

MOJO MUSTARD

1 cup (240 g) yellow mustard

1 tbsp (15 ml) honey

2 tsp (10 ml) chile paste

1 tsp minced fresh oregano

½ tsp ground cumin

Zest of 1 orange

1 tbsp (15 ml) fresh orange juice

Zest and juice of 1 lime

1 clove garlic, minced

Kosher salt, to taste

Freshly ground black pepper, to taste

SANDWICH

1 fresh Cuban long roll

2 slices Swiss cheese

Thinly sliced sweet pickles

4 oz (120 g) Lechon Pork Shoulder (page 177)

4 oz (120 g) carved pit-cured ham

Butter, as needed

To make the mojo mustard, in a medium bowl, mix together the mustard, honey, chile paste, oregano, cumin, orange zest, and juice, lime zest and juice, garlic, salt and pepper.

To make the sandwich, preheat a flat press or a large cast-iron skillet or griddle over medium heat.

Lay the bread, open side up, on a work surface and spread the bottom and top halves with 2 ounces (60 ml) of the mojo mustard. Place the Swiss cheese on top of the sauce. Working only on the bottom halves, layer all of the pickles, Lechon Pork Shoulder and cured ham. Close the sandwich, pressing gently.

Butter the top and bottom of the sandwich. Place it in the flat press and press the sandwich with moderate pressure until it is crisp on both sides, about 8 minutes. If you are using a cast-iron skillet or griddle, melt some butter in the skillet or on the griddle and add the sandwich. Use a second skillet to press on it as the first side crisps. When the first side is crisp, flip the sandwich. Add more butter, swirling the skillet to coat, and continue pressing until the sandwich is crisp on both sides, about 10 minutes.

Slice the sandwich in half diagonally and serve immediately.

GREENWITCH QUE CO.

GREENWICH, CONNECTICUT » JOHN AMBROGIO

@greenwitch_que_co on Instagram
greenwitchqueco@gmail.com

Since 2009, John and Greenwitch Que Co. have been serving up great barbecue to the folks of Fairfield County, Connecticut. From catering intimate events or feeding the masses at a festival, Greenwitch Que Co. has put the emphasis on the quality of their product and integrity. The first time I met John was at the Greenwich Town Party, s small-town get-together of about eight thousand people where John and his friend Corey Pieczko were competing against other barbecue teams (including mine) for top honors. As luck would have it, our spots were next to each other. We spent the night diving into each other's coolers and sharing barbecue stories as we monitored our fires. John and Corey went on to win the people's choice awards for best pork and best chicken at the Greenwich Town Party. Since then, I have had the pleasure of competing against Greenwitch Que Co. numerous times as they have racked up state championship awards in multiple states. In 2018, they were crowned the people's champions at the Mohegan Sun BBQ Fest. When not getting people out of tight situations as a locksmith, John caters for corporate clients and family gatherings. Be on the lookout for Greenwitch Que Co., as they have been known to pop up at various events and fundraisers.

SAUSAGE FATTY

Life is not complete without a savory fatty made on your barbecue. The bacon-wrapped stuffed Sausage Fatty is also called a bacon explosion on the internet. Around here, we just call it a fatty and everyone knows what we are talking about. If you have never tried eating or making one of these, you are in for a real treat. It is unbearably delicious and it's not nearly as difficult as it looks. The first time may not go quickly, but once you see the process, the lights will come on and the next one will go much faster and easier. Make a couple at a time—these have been known to be consumed in bulk by guests.

COOK TIME: 2 hours   **YIELD:** 10 to 12 servings

2 tbsp (30 ml) olive oil

1 red bell pepper, diced

1 yellow bell pepper, diced

1 orange bell pepper, diced

2 cloves garlic, minced

1 small yellow onion, diced

8 oz (240 g) hot Italian sausage

1 lb (450 g) sweet Italian sausage

1 lb (450 g) uncooked bacon

¼ cup (30 g) all-purpose barbecue dry rub, divided

3 slices Colby Jack cheese, cut in half

1 jalapeño, diced

1 cup (240 ml) barbecue sauce

Heat the oil in a large skillet over medium heat. Add the red bell pepper, yellow bell pepper, orange bell pepper, garlic and onion and cook until the garlic and onion are translucent, 3 minutes. Place the mixture in the refrigerator until it has cooled.

In a medium bowl, mix together the hot Italian sausage and sweet Italian sausage. Put the sausage mixture in a food storage bag and flatten it out until the mixture reaches all the edges of the bag and is of equal thickness throughout. Set the bag aside.

Construct a bacon weave on a cutting board with the uncooked bacon.

Cut open the bag of sausage, so one side is completely exposed. Flip the sausage over and place it on top of the bacon. Dust an even coating of about half of the barbecue dry rub on the sausage. Place the 6 halves of Colby Jack cheese evenly across the sausage. Sprinkle the sautéed bell pepper, garlic, and onion mixture on the cheese. Top that with the jalapeño.

Starting at the top of the cutting board, roll the sausage like a cinnamon roll. Then, starting at the bottom, roll the bacon weave around the sausage, forming it into a log. Sprinkle the log with the remaining barbecue dry rub.

Prepare the smoker to cook indirectly at 300°F (149°C), using hickory wood.

Place the Sausage Fatty on the grill grate and cook until it reaches an internal temperature of 165°F (74°C), about 2 hours. During the last 30 minutes of cooking, brush on the barbecue sauce.

Remove the Sausage Fatty from the smoker and let it rest for 30 minutes. Slice it into approximately 1-inch (2.5-cm) slices and serve.

A PITMASTER'S TOP FIVE SECRET WEAPONS

Emmert Wolf was once quoted as saying, "A man is only as good as his tools." This principle could be applied to a variety of disciplines, barbecue being one of them. Whether in our home, at a competition or in the restaurant, we barbecue fanatics are always reaching for something. From lighting your fire to getting your product off the pit, these are five tools of the trade to help you make better barbecue:

MAP GAS TORCHES

The optimized flame burns hot and efficiently for maximum heat output to light your charcoal fast. The auto start-stop ignition lights and extinguishes with the push of a button.

CHARCOAL CHIMNEYS

These are great for lighting charcoal. They are simple to use and a great alternative to using lighter fluid.

TEMPERATURE CONTROL DEVICES

Better known in the barbecue world as "Gurus," these devices usually have three parts: a fan, a thermometer and a control unit. The control unit monitors the temperature of your pit and controls the amount of air on your fire via the fan. Barbecue is all about time and temperature—when you have consistent temperature, you have a product of consistent quality. There are plenty of manufacturers of temperature control devices; however, I have only used a BBQ Guru device. Regardless of your pit, they have a device for you. Visit www.bbqguru.com to learn more.

DIGITAL THERMOMETERS

Having a thermometer is great, but having an accurate one is imperative to the cooking process. I highly recommend getting a digital thermometer. They give an accurate and instant read, saving time and allowing less heat to escape your cooker. Both ThermoWorks and Lavatools make thermometers I have used and approve of. Some come with features such as being backlit for taking temps at night or being magnetic so you don't lose it.

DREDGES OR SHAKERS

These are a necessity when applying your rub. They can be purchased in different sizes to suit your needs. I usually have three or four on hand. As you build your flavor profiles, you will develop layering your rubs on your meat.

BUTCH'S SMACK YOUR LIPS BBQ

MOUNT LAUREL, NEW JERSEY » ALYSON LUPINETTI AND MATT MEYER

P.O. Box 338

Mount Laurel, N J 08054

www.smackyourlipsbbq.com

Butch and Lynne Lupinetti owned a barbecue restaurant from 1970 to 1997 called Butch's Blues and BBQ in New Jersey. In 1982, Butch and Lynne stumbled on a rib cook-off and attended all day. They asked a ton of questions and by the end of the cook-off, they had purchased a smoker and began competing. And the rest is history. Butch found success on the competition trail, winning numerous awards (including the grand championship at the Jack Daniels World Championship Invitational Barbecue).

Today, you can find Butch's Smack Your Lips BBQ vending at some of the largest barbecue festivals. From Wildwood, New Jersey, to Reno, Nevada, they are serving insane amounts of high-quality barbecue. They are known for their ribs, and I can attest that the way they cook them sets them apart from their competition. As the ribs come out of the smoker, they put the ribs on the grill and mop them with a bit of their mild sauce while they grill them for several minutes. The grilling provides a bit of a crust on the ribs, which complements their tenderness. Butch's Smack Your Lips BBQ provides the ribs to their customers and lets them choose their sauce.

The legacy that Butch Lupinetti started with Butch's Smack Your Lips BBQ continues stronger than ever with Butch's daughter, Alyson, and her husband, Matt Meyer, leading the team. Don't worry—Lynne is usually close by, keeping an eye on quality control. Butch's Smack Your Lips BBQ has won more than six hundred awards, but more importantly, they are great people who make barbecue the right way. When you visit your local barbecue festival, look for the signature lips logo and get in line.

BONE-IN BOSTON BUTT PULLED PORK

Smoked pull pork takes time, so make sure you plan ahead to make this beauty from Butch's. A lot of people dread making pulled pork because they see the amount of time that goes into it. The big surprise is that it only takes 5 to 10 minutes to prep and the smoker does the rest. The inclusion of cherrywood to this recipe will give your bark great color and your meat a flavorful taste.

COOK TIME: 8 to 10 hours **YIELD:** 12 servings

1 (8-lb [3.6-kg]) bone-in Boston butt

¼ cup (30 g) Butch's Smack Your Lips BBQ Magic Dust seasoning rub

Prepare the smoker to cook indirectly at 225°F (107°C), using cherrywood.

Score the fat cap of the Boston butt through the fat only. Rub the meat liberally with the Butch's Smack Your Lips BBQ Magic Dust.

Cook the Boston butt until it reaches an internal temperature of 195°F (91°C), 8 to 10 hours.

If you are using the meat immediately, remove the bone by twisting it. It should come out easily. Slice the meat or use 2 forks to shred the meat. If you wish to use the meat later, wrap the butt in a double layer of foil to retain the juices and refrigerate or freeze it.

BUTCH'S CREAMY SLAW

In the world of barbecue, it is difficult to find items that go together better then pulled pork and coleslaw. From side dish to sandwich topper, a good slaw will always serve a purpose. Good barbecue needs sides the same way good blues needs rhythm.

YIELD: 12 servings

2 cups (680 g) finely shredded green cabbage

1 cup (340 g) finely shredded red cabbage

⅓ cup (73 g) mayonnaise

1 tbsp (15 ml) distilled white vinegar

2 tsp (8 g) sugar

½ tsp salt

½ tsp celery seeds

1 carrot, grated

¼ cup (50 g) minced onion

Place the green cabbage and red cabbage in ice water to keep them crisp until you are ready to toss the coleslaw.

In a large bowl, combine the mayonnaise, vinegar, sugar, salt and celery seeds. Stir until the sugar is dissolved.

Drain the cabbage and toss it together with the carrot, onion and mayonnaise mixture and serve.

See the image on page 184.

CORN BREAD

This classic sweet and easy corn bread makes a great side dish for breakfast, lunch or dinner. It might just be better than your grandma's recipe—but don't worry, we won't tell.

COOK TIME: 25 minutes   **YIELD:** 12 servings

1 cup (170 g) stone-ground cornmeal

¾ cup (94 g) unbleached all-purpose flour

2 tsp (8 g) baking powder

2 tbsp (24 g) sugar

½ cup (120 ml) canola oil

2 eggs

1 cup (121 g) sour cream or 1 cup (240 ml) buttermilk

1 cup (144 g) creamed corn (optional)

Preheat the oven to 375°F (191°C). Use a 9 x 9–inch (23 x 23–cm) bread pan or muffin tin lined with paper cups.

In a large bowl, combine the cornmeal, flour, baking powder and sugar. In another large bowl, combine the oil, eggs, sour cream and creamed corn, if using. Add the cornmeal mixture to the oil mixture and use a hand mixer to blend the two together. Allow the batter to rest for 10 minutes. The batter should be thick.

Pour the batter into the prepared pan and bake for 20 to 25 minutes, until the corn bread is golden brown in color and a toothpick inserted in the center comes out clean.

See the image on page 184.

RED WHITE & QUE SMOKEHOUSE

KEARNY, NEW JERSEY » DAN MISURACA

266 Davis Ave.
Kearny, NJ 07032
www.redwhiteandquesmokehouse.com

Red White & Que Smokehouse opened in 2016 and has been an indisputable success ever since. Within six months of opening, Dan and Katie Misuraca were being lauded by social and mainstream media for bringing great barbecue to Kearny, New Jersey. Brisket, ribs and homemade sausage are all musts when you visit. The Misuracas use quality cuts of meat and make just about everything by hand. The first time I met Dan and Katie, we were at an event showcasing our barbecue businesses. We tried to talk, but our lines were way too long to stop and have a conversation. I told Dan I would stop by and discuss a project I was working on (this book). I'm so glad I followed up.

Red White & Que Smokehouse is a patriotic barbecue restaurant that far exceeds the name. As you enter Red White & Que Smokehouse, you are greeted with American and Marine Corps flags and the beautiful sight of their J&R Manufacturing Little Red Smokehouse.

Dan, a former marine who served in Kuwait during the Gulf War, feels strongly about supporting and helping our veterans. The couple has partnered with veterans' organizations throughout New Jersey to contribute meals to veterans in need. They offer the Red White & Que Smokehouse "Buy a Vet a Meal" program: Customers can buy a meal or make a monetary donation, which the Misuracas will use to feed a veteran. Periodically, they will also hold pig-roast fund-raisers where, for a nominal fee, you get a heaping plate of pork and sides with all the monies being donated to various veteran charities, from Veterans Administration hospitals to Veterans of Foreign Wars.

Three things you must do when you visit Red White & Que Smokehouse: (1) order some brisket, (2) order some collard greens (3) and buy a vet a meal. Your stomach and your heart will feel better at the end. God bless barbecue. God bless America. Thank you, Dan and Katie Misuraca. Semper fi.

MAPLE-CURED BACON

How can I begin to tell you how phenomenally easy it is to make your own homemade bacon? Actually, I don't have to because Dan has given us his recipe for maple-cured bacon. Homemade bacon is different from the wet mush in stores. There is a true smoked flavor, and in this particular recipe, there are sweet maple high notes and a hint of pepper. You've heard this a million times, but it's crucial to find a great butcher, one who can get you a nice piece of pork belly. Curing bacon takes several days, so you'll need to prepare in advance, but it's well worth the wait.

COOK TIME: 3 hours   **YIELD:** 7 lb (3.1 kg) slab bacon

1 (10-lb [4.5-kg]) pork belly

¼ cup (60 ml) pure maple syrup

¼ cup (72 g) kosher salt

2 tsp (10 g) pink curing salt

½ cup (56 g) butcher-grind black pepper, divided

¼ cup (36 g) dark brown sugar

2 tbsp (16 g) red pepper flakes

2 tbsp (18 g) sweet paprika

Remove the skin from the pork belly, then trim any excess fat and cut off the ends to square it off. After trimming, the pork belly will be about 7 pounds (3.1 kg). Rinse the trimmed pork belly and pat it dry.

Coat the pork belly with the maple syrup.

In a large bowl, combine the kosher salt, pink curing salt, ¼ cup (28 g) of black pepper, brown sugar, red pepper flakes and paprika. Coat the pork belly with this seasoning mix.

Place the seasoned pork belly in a resealable freezer bag. Seal and refrigerate it for 7 days, flipping once a day until the pork belly feels firm. Remove the pork belly from the freezer bag and rinse it thoroughly to remove any excess seasoning, then pat it dry. Place the pork belly on a wire rack and refrigerate it, uncovered, for 48 hours.

Prepare the smoker to cook at 200°F (93°C), using hickory wood (note that any wood will do).

Coat the cured bacon with the remaining ¼ cup (28 g) of black pepper. Place the bacon in the smoker and cook for 3 hours, or until the bacon reaches an internal temperature of 150°F (66°F).

Slice the bacon thickly thinly and panfry as desired.

HAM HOCK COLLARD GREENS

We all have the one side dish that is pretty much our Southern favorite. It just so happens that collard greens are mine. Collard greens are a Southern classic, regardless of how they're prepared, but this recipe from Dan is the easiest way I've ever gone about cooking them. Cooking the greens and ham hocks on low for four hours ensures that all the flavors meld together beautifully. Starting the dish with onion and garlic as the base and then adding ham hocks creates a very tasty cooking liquid for the greens. The smokiness infuses the broth with a deep, complex taste and the ham hocks certainly don't hurt.

COOK TIME: 4 hours   **YIELD:** 15 servings

½ cup (76 g) minced garlic

¼ cup (32 g) red pepper flakes

¾ cup (180 g) salt

½ cup (60 g) granulated garlic

½ cup (60 g) granulated onion

2 cups (480 ml) distilled white vinegar

2 whole smoked ham hocks

5 lb (2.3 kg) trimmed and washed collard greens

1 yellow onion, chopped

Water, as needed

In a large pot over medium-high heat, combine the minced garlic, red pepper flakes, salt, granulated garlic, granulated onion, vinegar, ham hocks, collard greens and onion. Fill the pot with water until all the ingredients are covered by 1 inch (2.5 cm).

Cook for at least 4 hours. The greens should be tender with a little bite, not mushy.

Remove the whole ham hocks from the pot to remove all of the meat. The meat should easily fall off the bone. Transfer the meat back to the pot with the cooked greens. Discard the ham bones.

JACK'S DOWNHOME BBQ

PHILADELPHIA, PENNSYLVANIA » JACK MCDAVID

Pitmaster Jack McDavid knows his way around a barbecue. With a résumé that includes hosting the Food Network's *Grillin' and Chillin'*, six James Beard invitations and winning the Whole Hog World Championship at Memphis in May, Jack McDavid has some serious cooking chops. From his distinctive Southern drawl to his trademark duds—denim bib overalls and a red and white trucker's cap heralding "Save the Farm"—Jack McDavid is a "good ol' boy" with a unique recipe for success. Jack decided on a career as a chef, honing skills in more than 115 restaurants during the 1970s and early 1980s. He learned classical French technique, as well as discipline, at Washington, DC's, bastion of French cuisine, Le Lion d'Or. However, it was the love of cooking barbecue with his grandfather in the mountains of Virginia that Jack couldn't shake. Jack opened his first restaurant, the Down Home Diner, in March 1987, at the Reading Terminal Market in Philadelphia. He wowed patrons with inexpensive, inventive dishes like corn bread pizza with Tennessee ham and chicken-fried buffalo steak with red-eye gravy. In November 1989, he opened Jack's Firehouse in the Fairmount area of Philadelphia, featuring "haute country" cuisine. In addition, he started Jack's Downhome BBQ, serving award-winning barbecue to patrons of some of largest barbecue festivals on the East Coast.

I had the pleasure of working an event where my company was the local barbecue vendor, along with Jack and others from outside the area. The organizer asked the vendors to make some ribs to take to the local radio stations. It was about 3:00 a.m. when I heard someone whistling and singing in the dark. It was Jack—he was showing up to light his smoker and make his ribs. I said good morning and startled the legend a bit.

"What are you doing here, kid?" he asked (I was thirty-six). I replied that I was making my ribs for the radio station event. "Hell, son, I thought I was the only one who makes their ribs from scratch. Some of these other vendors have premade product they are reheating." I told him that was not how I was raised and that I made all of our product and made them fresh. He asked if I had room on my smoker for a couple more racks. Of course I did—this was Jack McDavid asking to use my pit. We spent the next three-plus hours talking about barbecue (actually, he talked and I listened). We tried each other's ribs before we went to the radio station and I felt like I had impressed the legend. It wasn't until we were at the radio station doing a plug when Jack told everyone that if they wanted to change their lives, they should try my ribs. I had earned the respect of a legend. Jack makes some of the best ribs and pulled pork you can find at an event. Get a side of slaw, as it has a sweetness that cuts the acid of the pork and vinegar sauce nicely.

CAST-IRON CORN BREAD
WITH HONEY BUTTER

One of the largest debates in all of barbecue might not have anything to do with meat at all. There are more variations, preferences and recipes for corn bread than practically all other barbecue foods combined. Jack is happy to give you a recipe for corn bread with honey butter to settle all differences. Toss that boxed mix in the garbage and make this easy homemade corn bread, which makes a great side dish.

COOK TIME: 25 to 30 minutes   **YIELD:** 12 servings

HONEY BUTTER
8 tbsp (120 g) butter, softened

3 tbsp (45 ml) honey

1 tbsp (8 g) powdered sugar

CORN BREAD
2 cups (250 g) all-purpose flour

1 cup (170 g) cornmeal

1 tbsp (12 g) baking powder

1 tsp salt

⅔ cup (128 g) sugar

½ cup plus 1 tbsp butter (130 g), softened, divided

1 tsp vanilla extract

2 large eggs

2 cups (480 ml) buttermilk

To make the honey butter, combine the butter, honey and powdered sugar in a medium bowl. Beat for 3 minutes using a hand mixer on low speed until the mixture is light and fluffy. Transfer the honey butter to a small bowl and refrigerate it until ready to use.

Preheat the barbecue to 350°F (177°C).

To make the corn bread, combine the flour, cornmeal, baking powder and salt in a medium bowl and set it aside.

Place the sugar, ½ cup (115 g) of the butter and vanilla in a medium bowl. Mix with a hand mixer until well combined. Add the eggs, one at a time, and continue mixing until the ingredients are well incorporated.

Stir the flour mixture and buttermilk, alternatingly, into the sugar mixture with a spoon until just combined.

Melt the remaining 1 tablespoon (15 g) of butter in a 10- to 12-inch (25- to 30-cm) cast-iron skillet over medium-high heat. When the butter has melted, remove the skillet from the heat and swirl the butter around to evenly coat the bottom of the skillet. Pour the corn bread batter into the skillet and place it in the barbecue.

Bake the corn bread for 25 to 30 minutes, or until a toothpick inserted in the center comes out clean. The exact baking time will depend on the size of the skillet, so watch the corn bread closely toward the end of the baking time.

POTATO SALAD

Is there anything better than a fresh potato salad at a barbecue? This potato salad is smoky, spicy and Southern goodness all rolled into one. By smoking the potatoes, another layer of flavor is created that will garner praise from your guests.

COOK TIME: 35 to 40 minutes   **YIELD:** 8 servings

2 lb (900 g) small red potatoes

3 tbsp (45 ml) olive oil

1 tbsp (18 g) kosher salt

1 tsp freshly ground black pepper

4 tbsp (60 ml) Sriracha sauce

1½ cups (330 g) mayonnaise

1 tbsp (3 g) finely chopped fresh parsley

1 tbsp (3 g) finely chopped scallions

In a large bowl, combine the potatoes, oil, salt and pepper. Toss the potatoes gently to coat them. Arrange the potatoes in a single layer in a large aluminum foil pan.

Prepare the smoker to cook indirectly at 275°F (135°C), using cherrywood.

Place the potatoes in the smoker and smoke until they are tender, 35 to 40 minutes. Stir the potatoes a couple of times during the smoking process so they brown evenly. Remove the potatoes and let them cool slightly (they should be warm).

While the potatoes are cooking, combine the Sriracha and mayonnaise in a large bowl. When the potatoes are cool to the touch, toss them with the Sriracha mayonnaise, parsley and scallions. Serve.

MAX CITY BBQ

LOS ANGELES, CALIFORNIA » JASON MCDONALD

4729 Eagle Rock Blvd.
Los Angeles, CA 90041
www.maxcitybbq.com

So you and your buddies are in the backyard pulling some barbecue off the smoker when one of your friends says, "This barbecue is great. You need to open a restaurant." Yeah, you've catered a few events but you have no experience running a restaurant and no capital. "That's easy," your buddy says. "We'll do a Kickstarter." That is exactly what cofounder and pitmaster Jason McDonald did.

Since opening their doors in 2014, Max City BBQ has been paying the public back with killer Southern-style 'cue. The corner location might not seat many; however, the food is worth sharing a table with a stranger. The barbecue chicken was full of flavor and moist. The St. Louis ribs were falling off the bone and comparable in flavor to what you would find in the Midwest. The mac 'n' cheese, corn bread and cucumber salad were my sides of choice. All were great, but the cucumber salad stood out. Jason told me it is a family recipe that has been passed down to him.

Max City BBQ keeps a rotating list of craft brews and signature selections of wine. You will find yourself spending as much time reviewing the beverages as you do the food. The homemade lemonade is excellent on a hot day.

SMOKED TRI-TIP

The tri-tip roast or steak (also called a triangle roast) is the 1½ to 2½ pounds (680 to 1100 g) of meat that sits at the bottom of the sirloin. For years, the beef tri-tip found itself being ground into hamburger or cut into cubes and sold as soup meat. Tri-tip is quite popular in the Central Coast and the Central Valley regions of California. It has begun to enjoy increasing favor elsewhere as well, for its full flavor, lower fat content and comparatively lower cost. Jason shares with us the recipe they use at Max City BBQ for their tri-tip.

COOK TIME: 1 hour **YIELD:** 6 servings

4 tbsp (24 g) freshly ground black pepper

3 tbsp (45 g) salt

½ tbsp (5 g) chili powder

1½ tbsp (14 g) brown sugar

1½ tbsp (14 g) onion powder

1 tbsp (9 g) ground mustard

1 tbsp (9 g) garlic powder

1 (3-lb [1.4-kg]) tri-tip steak

½ cup (120 ml) apple juice

½ cup (120 ml) apple cider vinegar

In a large bowl, combine the pepper, salt, chili powder, brown sugar, onion powder, ground mustard and garlic powder. Rub this mixture evenly over the tri-tip.

In a food-safe spray bottle, combine the apple juice and vinegar. Set it aside.

Prepare the smoker to cook indirectly at 250°F (121°C), using oak and hickory wood. Place the tri-tip on the smoker and cook until the internal temperature is 125°F (52°C), about 60 minutes. Spray the tri-tip every 25 minutes with the juice-vinegar mixture.

Remove the tri-tip from the smoker and let the meat rest. Meanwhile, prepare the smoker to cook directly over the coals.

Place the tri-tip directly over the coals for approximately 3 minutes per side to sear the outside. The internal temperature should be 135°F (57°C).

Let the tri-tip rest for 15 minutes and slice it across the grain.

MAC 'N' CHEESE

Jason makes one of the cheesiest mac 'n' cheeses I've ever had. When I asked for the recipe, he was a bit hesitant but finally caved in to my constant requests. This five-cheese bowl of heaven is something you will find yourself making on numerous occasions. It is nothing short of phenomenal.

COOK TIME: 25 to 30 minutes   **YIELD:** 12 servings

½ cup (120 ml) whole milk

3 cups (720 ml) heavy cream

¾ cup (94 g) all-purpose flour

1 lb (450 g) sharp cheddar cheese, shredded

½ lb (225 g) white cheddar cheese, shredded

½ lb (225 g) fontina cheese, shredded

½ lb (225 g) Velveeta processed cheese product

¾ cup (135 g) grated Parmesan cheese

2 lb (900 g) cooked elbow macaroni

Preheat the oven to 400°F (204°C).

In a large pot over medium heat, bring the milk and heavy cream to a simmer. Slowly whisk in the flour and simmer until the mixture thickens, whisking constantly, about 5 minutes.

Slowly add the sharp cheddar cheese, white cheddar cheese, fontina cheese, Velveeta and Parmesan cheese, stirring so all the cheeses are evenly distributed.

Once all the cheeses have melted, add the macaroni to the pot and stir to combine it with the cheese mixture.

Place macaroni and cheese into a half-size aluminum steam tray and bake for 25 to 30 minutes.

See the image on page 200.

KLOBY'S SMOKEHOUSE

LAUREL, MARYLAND » **STEVE KLOBOSITS**

7500 Montpelier Rd.
Laurel, MD 20723
www.klobysbbq.com

As my family and I started to head south on our barbecue journey, it didn't take long before all the talk about food in the car made us hungry. A quick search by the navigator revealed we were in proximity of Kloby's Smokehouse in Laurel, Maryland. And what a gem is Kloby's.

A festive mood greeted us as faithful Baltimore Orioles fans cheered on their team over their barbecue. I was excited to see a menu that has something for everyone—from traditional barbecue to creative dishes like a bourbon-cured salmon salad, a brisket cheesesteak and Kloby's trademarked Jar-B-Que (a layer of pulled pork, barbecue beans and coleslaw served in a mason jar and topped with a pickled green tomato). Their drink menu is as impressive as their food menu, with forty different bourbons and rye whiskeys available and as many drafts on tap.

Owner Steve Klobosits told me he opened Kloby's in 2008 as a counter-service barbecue joint. Today, Kloby's is a full-service restaurant and bar. Steve stated he'd always had a passion for cooking and that after many years working as a paramedic and firefighter, he enrolled at a restaurant school to earn his culinary degree. Much of the decor of Kloby's pays homage to his past in public service.

The day starts early at Kloby's as all items are made on the premise from recipes that Steve has created. I enjoyed some Sweet Bourbon Wings, hush puppies and the Carolina-Style Pulled Pork Sandwich. I'd be hard-pressed to decide which was my favorite—I might need to make another trip to Kloby's to find out.

BOURBON-CURED SMOKED SALMON

There's no healthier, easier or faster summer entrée than a piece of grilled salmon. This recipe from Kloby's should be a staple in your dinner routine. There is just enough smokiness to the fish that it is not overwhelming, while the cure of the sugar and bourbon give the salmon a great balance of flavor.

COOK TIME: 45 minutes   **YIELD:** 6 to 8 servings

1 cup (240 ml) bourbon

1 cup (144 g) brown sugar

1 cup (240 ml) water

¼ cup (72 g) kosher salt

1 tbsp (6 g) freshly ground black pepper

1 (3- to 4-lb [1.4- to 1.8-kg]) fresh skin-off salmon

Combine the bourbon, brown sugar, water, salt and pepper in a pot. Bring the mixture to a boil. Remove the mixture from the heat and let it cool. Lay the salmon flat in a large shallow baking pan and pour the cold cure over the salmon and refrigerate it overnight.

Prepare the smoker for indirect cooking at 225°F (107°C), using apple or other fruit wood. Note that seafood is a sponge for smoke. Start with minimal wood until you find the amount that is acceptable to you.

Allow the salmon to come to room temperature. Place the salmon on a baking rack over a baking sheet and smoke until the salmon reaches an internal temperature of 165°F (74°C), about 45 minutes or until the salmon flakes apart.

SMOKED CORNED BEEF

Not much beats corned beef for a Saint Paddy's Day meal, and this recipe for smoked corned beef brisket will top any other. Steve shares with us a smoked corned beef to enjoy for the holidays. This is an amazing twist to corned beef that I highly recommend trying. I usually prepare two so I have the extra to throw on the meat slicer for thinly sliced sandwich meat.

COOK TIME: 10 to 12 hours   **YIELD:** 15 servings

1 cup (120 g) Cajun seasoning

1½ cups (216 g) brown sugar

1 (10- to 12-lb [4.5- to 5.4-kg]) raw whole corned beef

4 cups (960 ml) apple juice

1 cup (240 ml) Irish whiskey

In a medium bowl, combine the Cajun seasoning and brown sugar. Rub this mixture over the entire corned beef and refrigerate the corned beef overnight.

Prepare the smoker for indirect cooking at 225°F (107°C), using about 4 large chunks of apple or other fruit wood.

Place the corned beef in a deep pan large enough for the brisket and liquid. Add the apple juice and Irish whiskey.

Smoke the corned beef until it reaches an internal temperature of 195°F (91°C), approximately 1 hour per pound, basting it with the drippings several times throughout the cooking process.

Once the desired internal temperature is reached, remove the corned beef from the smoker and let it rest for 30 minutes before slicing.

OLD VIRGINIA SMOKE

BRISTOW, VIRGINIA » LUKE DARNELL

www.oldvirginiasmoke.com

Luke Darnell began cooking on a Brinkmann electric bullet and then got the fever. Several years and smokers later, he had the opportunity to join a competitive barbecue team, Smoke Dreams BBQ. Rather than just joining and learning the ropes, Luke went out and bought a Weber Smokey Mountain Cooker right out of the gate. After a couple years under the tutelage of Smoke Dreams BBQ pitmaster Kirk learning the ins and outs of competitive barbecue, it was time for Luke to introduce the world to Old Virginia Smoke. Since 2013, with the help of his wife, Kimberly, Old Virginia Smoke has amassed an impressive number of awards. In 2016, Luke was named world barbecue champion at the World Food Championships. Old Virginia Smoke was named the KCBS Team of the Year for Grand Champion for Chicken in 2017. It is not only the multiple grand championships and reserved championships (second place at barbecue competitions) that they have won; it is the consistency with which they do it: From Rochester, New York, to Rocky Mount, North Carolina, this team always brings their A game, impressively finishing in the top ten 70 percent of the time they compete.

One of the things that Luke likes the most about competitive barbecue is the support of his fellow competitors. For the most part, we barbecue folks are people from all walks of life. Yet some of the people who will be your best and oldest friends will be barbecue people. From forgetting something at home to the unfortunate circumstance of breaking down on the side of the road, it is someone from your barbecue family who is going to lend a hand. We are happy when our friends succeed, just as they are when our name is called.

ST. LOUIS RIBS

A KCBS barbecue contest is a four-category, blind-judge event. Six judges try your product and score it based on appearance, taste and tenderness. Each judge takes one bite and scores accordingly, with a 9 in each category being the highest score. Of the four categories (chicken, ribs, pork and brisket), the category with typically the closest margin of scoring is ribs. The Old Virginia Smoke team is consistently at the top of the list for their ribs. Luke has shared their competition recipe with us and it is a proven winner, whether it's on the judges' table or the dinner table.

COOK TIME: 3 to 3½ hours   **YIELD:** 4 (½-rack) servings

2 (2½- to 3-lb [1.1- to 1.4-kg]) racks Smithfield Extra Tender Fresh Pork St. Louis Style Spareribs

Smokin' Guns BBQ hot rub, as needed

Big Poppa Smokers Sweet Money barbecue rub, as needed

1 (12-oz [360-ml]) bottle spray butter

½ cup (72 g) brown sugar, divided

1 stick (120 g) Challenge brand butter, sliced lengthwise, divided

½ cup (120 ml) honey

Prepare the smoker for indirect cooking at 275°F (135°C), using hickory wood.

Trim the ribs, squaring up both sides and removing the membrane off of the back of the ribs. Season the back of the ribs moderately with the Smokin' Guns rub. Then add a generous coat of the Big Poppa Smokers Sweet Money rub. Let the ribs sit for 30 minutes, and then repeat this process on the meat side.

Spray the ribs with spray butter and put them into the smoker for 1 hour. After 1 hour, add another chunk of hickory wood and spray the ribs with the spray butter again. Cook for 1 hour.

Remove the ribs from the smoker and lay out 4 large pieces of foil. On the foil, create a bed of ¼ cup (36 g) of the brown sugar, 2 slices of the butter and the honey. Put the ribs on the foil, meat side down. Add the remaining ¼ cup (36 g) of brown sugar and 1 slice of butter to the back of the ribs. Wrap the ribs tightly with a second piece of foil, and smoke for 1 to 1½ hours.

The ribs will be done when you see some end bones popping out and the internal temperature is between 202 and 205°F (94 and 96°C).

5 ALARM
BACKYARD BBQ

TEANECK, NEW JERSEY » CURTIS BARNES

www.5alarmbbq.net

The first time I met Curtis Barnes, he and his team were catering an outing at an upscale private country club. To be honest, I was skeptical when the club organizers said we were having barbecue for dinner. When I realized this barbecue was the real deal, I walked around back to find out where it came from. This was not the bake-your-brisket-in-the-oven-with-liquid-smoke fare that I was expecting at a country club.

The following week, Curtis's and my teams were at a KCBS competition in Cresskill, New Jersey, where the 5 Alarm Backyard BBQ team took top honors for ribs. As you may have guessed by now, with a team name of 5 Alarm Backyard BBQ, Curtis is a firefighter. In addition, he is the NYC lead for Operation BBQ Relief, a nonprofit disaster relief organization that provides hot barbecue meals to those affected by disasters and the first responders helping them. Curtis is one of the most selfless people I know and a very talented pitmaster. The 5 Alarm Backyard BBQ team has traveled from Rhode Island to North Carolina, competing and providing concessions. If you see the 5 Alarm Backyard BBQ rig, do yourself a favor and get something to eat. With his trademark smile and smoked sticky wings, Curtis will feed you like family.

SMOKED STICKY WINGS

These sticky wings are the perfect item for cocktail parties or tailgating. The cherry-smoke flavor and honey make these wings irresistible.

COOK TIME: 35 minutes   **YIELD**: 10 servings

2 cups (480 ml) honey

2 cups (480 ml) barbecue sauce

½ cup (60 g) barbecue dry rub

5 lb (2.3 kg) chicken drumettes or wings

4 cups (960 ml) peanut oil

In a large bowl, combine the honey and barbecue sauce. Mix them thoroughly and set it aside.

Prepare the smoker to cook directly at 250°F (121°C), adding 2 chunks of cherrywood to the hot coals.

Gently apply a light layer of dry rub to the drumettes. Place them on the grill and smoke for about 25 minutes. They should have a red color to them from the smoke. Do not let allow them to cook fully.

With the drumettes still on the grill, increase the temperature of the fire to 375°F (191°C). Heat the peanut oil to 325°F (163°C) in a 7-quart (6.7-L) Dutch oven.

Place the drumettes in the oil and fry them until they're fully cooked, 10 to 12 minutes. Generally, they will start to float to the surface of the oil when they are done. Drain the excess oil from the drumettes.

Toss the drumettes with the honey–barbecue sauce mixture until they are evenly covered. Serve hot.

HANDSOME DEVIL BBQ

NEWBURGH, NEW YORK » ED RANDOLPH

404 Lake Osiris Road
Walden, NY 12586
www.handsomedevilllc.com

As you peruse the book, we have shared stories and restaurants of pitmasters from all walks of life. From those with barbecue born into their DNA to software engineers and accountants. The one thing we all have is a passion for barbecue—to be able to share our craft and make sure that it carries on for generations to come. I've have been blessed with the ability to do what I enjoy and travel. While BBQ is regional and everyone within that region has their alliance, I am here to tell you that wherever you travel you can find great BBQ.

I had the pleasure of traveling this summer with my wife and daughters as we did a BBQ tour of the Southeast. Granted, I am not sure how I convinced the four of them to spend their summer vacation going from state to state to eat BBQ, I have a feeling there will be retribution in my future. However, there really are few things better than being able to see the world through a child's eyes. If you ask my girls about the trip today, they probably mention the comeback sauce at Ubons or how Emma ate ten different items at Fox Bros., but they will also talk about the people. How everyone treated us like family, were respectful and helpful. When we were at Lewis Barbecue in Charleston, Ben, the manager, was helping us with dinner reservations. At that point my oldest, Lily, looked and said, "Daddy, how do all these people know us? They are all so nice." Maybe it would be the same with other cuisine. But deep down I really feel it is the world of BBQ that is special. That no matter where you are from or where you are going, you are family. In a time where we are all running in opposite directions with our phones in our hands, we need to remember to step back and remember what is important. There is something to be said for piling the kids in the car and driving from Atlanta to Nashville to Biloxi. It would not have been uncommon a decade ago. However, there were zero complaints; we made a pact that if we saw something worth stopping, you just had to say, "Stop." From underground caverns to roadside ice cream stands, we did everything as a family and made memories none of us will forget.

In the BBQ world, the HD crew has accomplished a lot in a short amount of time. We have taken a startup company to multistate BBQ championship award winner to being the feature vendor at the Memphis in May World Barbecue Championships. In 2017, we were voted Best Barbecue at the Food Network Wine and Food Festival. In 2018, we won the NJ BBQ Showdown, were voted Best BBQ in the Hudson Valley, became a finalist for best food truck by the NY Beef Council and were asked to participate in the NYC Wine and Food Festival and the South Beach Wine and Food Festival presented by the Food Network. I love to cook with my children. The fact that all my girls enjoy being in the kitchen or by the smoker means the world to me. From pizza to prime rib, it is amazing to watch how each has a different strength. Lily can lay a coat of rub with precise coverage, Emma manhandles meat like a butcher and little Miss Amai can whisk a béchamel sauce into shape better than most Italian restaurants. Next time you're preparing to make dinner, ask your child if they want to help. Might be the most fun you've had in the kitchen in a while.

DEVIL'S SMOKED MAC 'N' CHEESE

When I started our company, there were five recipes that I wanted to create to identify our brand: three sauces, a base rub and a killer macaroni and cheese. We are really proud of our mac 'n' cheese. We feel the cheese mixture bonds to the *cavatappi* pasta better than to traditional elbow macaroni.

COOK TIME: 40 minutes   **YIELD**: 12 servings

6 tbsp (90 g) unsalted butter

6 tbsp (54 g) all-purpose flour

4 cups (960 ml) milk

1¼ cups (151 g) sour cream

1½ tsp (8 g) salt

3¾ cups (416 g) shredded mozzarella cheese, divided

1¾ cups (212 g) shredded aged cheddar cheese, divided

1 lb (450 g) cooked cavatappi pasta, at room temperature

1 cup (121 g) dried breadcrumbs

In a large pot over medium heat, melt the butter. Add the flour, whisking until it is incorporated. Add the milk, bring the mixture to a simmer and whisk until thick, 15 minutes. Add the sour cream and salt. Bring the mixture to a simmer. Remove it from the heat and stir in 1¼ cups (139 g) of the mozzarella cheese and 1¼ cups (151 g) of the aged cheddar cheese.

Prepare the smoker to cook indirectly at 350°F (177°C). Feel free to experiment with wood if you would like a smoke profile. We prefer lump charcoal.

Combine the pasta and cheese sauce. Stir in the remaining 2½ cups (277 g) of mozzarella cheese and the remaining ½ cup (61 g) of aged cheddar cheese. Top the pasta with the breadcrumbs and cook for 40 minutes.

KCBS COMPETITION CHICKEN

Competition barbecue is all about six people taking one bite of your food. That one bite needs to be tender and flavorful. The Handsome Devil team has worked hard on our chicken recipe and we are proud of the state championship calls it has given us.

COOK TIME: 2½ hours   **YIELD**: 16 servings

CHICKEN

16 bone-in, skin-on chicken thighs (see Tip)

Smokin' Guns Hot Rub, as needed

Meat Church BBQ Honey Hog BBQ rub, as needed

2 (12-oz [360-ml]) bottles spray butter

BRINE

¾ cup (180 g) Smoky Okie's The Solution soluble brine

3 cups (720 ml) water

To make the chicken, carefully peel and remove the skin from a chicken thigh. Trim the fat that runs alongside the thigh and remove the large knuckle. Slice the other knuckle to square up the thigh. The thigh should be about 2¼ inches (6 cm) wide. Trim the skin to make it square. Place the skin back on the chicken thigh and place it in a 2-gallon (8 L) sealable freezer bag. Repeat this process with the remaining chicken thighs.

To make the brine, combine the Smoky Okie's The Solution soluble brine and water in a large measuring cup. Pour the brine into the freezer bag over the chicken thighs and refrigerate overnight.

Put the brined chicken thighs on paper towels to drain. Pat the chicken thighs to remove any excess brine. On a work surface, arrange the thighs, bottom side up with the skins spread out. Shake a layer of Smokin' Guns Hot Rub onto the bottoms of each piece. Shake a layer of the Meat Church BBQ Honey Hog BBQ rub on the bottoms of each piece. Flip the pieces over and repeat this process on the top side. Place the thighs in the skins and wrap them up. Liberally season the tops of the pieces with the Smokin' Guns Hot Rub and Meat Church BBQ Honey Hog BBQ rub. Place the chicken in 2 half-size aluminum steam pans in 2 rows of 4 pieces in each pan.

Prepare the smoker to cook indirectly at 275°F (135°C), using cherrywood.

Pour a bottle of liquid butter into each pan around and between the chicken thighs, making sure not to wash off any of the rub. Place the chicken thighs in the smoker and cook for 1½ hours.

(continued)

SAUCE

2¾ cups (660 ml) Blues Hog Original BBQ Sauce

¾ cup (180 ml) BBQ Bob's Hav-N-BBQ original sauce

¾ cup (180 ml) Blues Hog Tennessee Red Sauce

Flip chicken thighs in the butter bath and cover the pans tightly with foil and place them back in the smoker. Cook for 45 minutes. Remove the foil from the pans. Liberally shake the Honey Hog rub onto the chicken thighs. Take them out of the butter bath and place them into a clean half pan. Shake the Honey Hog rub onto the tops of the chicken thighs. Repeat this process with the second pan of chicken thighs, using only one rack. Return the thighs to the top rack of the smoker for 15 minutes.

Meanwhile, make the sauce by combining the Blues Hog Original, BBQ Bob's Hav-N-BBQ and Blues Hog Tennessee Red sauces in a large bowl.

Remove the chicken thighs from the smoker and dip each piece into the chicken sauce. Place the chicken thighs back into the smoker. Let the sauce set for 10 minutes, then remove the chicken thighs from the smoker and serve.

TIP: *When purchasing your chicken, make sure it is white, not yellow.*

ANGRY ORCHARD WHITE CHOCOLATE CHEESECAKE

While I love barbecue, the devil also has a huge sweet tooth. It wasn't long after I fired up my pits that I was working on recipes to make a dessert on the barbecue. Then my friends at Angry Orchard asked me to incorporate their cider into my recipes for a special event. The combination of their Crisp Apple hard cider in my white chocolate cheesecake was a home run. This recipe has won numerous awards in competitions.

COOK TIME: 50 minutes   **YIELD**: 8 servings

CRUST
5 oz (148 ml) melted butter

1⅓ cups (120 g) graham cracker crumbs

FILLING
7 oz (210 g) white chocolate

1 cup (240 ml) Angry Orchard Crisp Apple hard cider

3 (8-oz [240-g]) packages cream cheese, at room temperature

1¼ cups (240 g) sugar

3 large eggs

2 tbsp (18 g) all-purpose flour

Prepare the smoker to cook indirectly at 350°F (177°C). Cut parchment paper to fit the bottom of a 9-inch (23-cm) cake pan. Spray the inside of the cake pan with nonstick cooking spray.

To make the crust, mix together the melted butter and graham cracker crumbs in a medium bowl. With your fingers, form a thin layer of the graham cracker mixture in the bottom and along the sides of the cake pan. Bake the crust in the smoker for 10 minutes.

To make the filling, heat the white chocolate in a double boiler on the stove over medium heat until it is completely melted. Add the hard cider to the melted chocolate. Set the white chocolate mixture aside to cool.

In a stand mixer fitted with the paddle attachment, combine the cream cheese and sugar on medium speed until the ingredients are completely incorporated. Keeping the mixer at medium speed, slowly add 1 egg at a time, scraping the sides of the bowl between each addition. Add the cooled white chocolate mixture. Slowly add the flour. Increase the speed to high to combine the ingredients.

Pour the filling into the baked crust. Place the cake pan in the middle of a 12 x 20–inch (30 x 50–cm) pan that is 2 inches (5 cm) deep. Fill the pan with warm water until it is within ½ inch (13 mm) from the top of the cake pan. Bake in the smoker for 40 minutes. Refrigerate the baked cheesecake.

(continued)

ANGRY ORCHARD WHITE CHOCOLATE CHEESECAKE (CONTINUED)

GANACHE

4 oz (120 g) white chocolate

¼ cup (60 ml) heavy cream

MAPLE WHIPPED CREAM

½ cup (120 ml) heavy cream

2 tsp (8 g) sugar

Pure maple syrup, to taste

To make the ganache, melt the white chocolate in a double boiler on the stove over medium heat and whip the heavy cream for 3 minutes, until it is thick. Spread a thin, even layer of ganache on top of the chilled cheesecake and refrigerate the cheesecake until the ganache has set.

To make the maple whipped cream, whip the cream and sugar together with a whisk or hand mixer for 4 minutes, or until soft peaks form. Add the maple syrup.

Slice the cheesecake and add a dollop of maple whipped cream to each slice before serving.

4050 Pennsylvania Ave., #150
Kansas City, MO 64111
www.charbarkc.com

The folks at Char Bar have created a new kind of barbecue playground. The environment is nothing short of amusing. A traditional barbecue joint with a red brick facade and hardwood floor, the restaurant boasts a large outdoor beer garden with games such as cornhole, bocce and croquet.

The menu at Char Bar is as pleasing as their atmosphere. Pitmaster Mitch Benjamin and executive chef Jeremy Tawney offer some of the best Southern-inspired traditional creations in addition to smokehouse vegetarian options to satisfy everyone who visits. Mitch Benjamin (a.k.a. Meat Mitch) is also the leader of a world championship–winning competition barbecue team from Kansas City. After more than a decade of honing his craft, Mitch and his smoking team created their own all-natural, unique array of spices and sauces specifically designed to win championships. The same sauces and rubs served at Char Bar can be found at www.meatmitch.com.

I happened to visit Char Bar on a Sunday when the special was the Char Bar fried chicken, served with whipped potatoes, gravy and a biscuit with TABASCO® honey. It was a wonderful fried chicken dinner, but I needed to try the burnt ends and hush puppies that others in the restaurant were raving about. Before I could try the beer that was dropped off at my table, I was handed a burnt-heaven sandwich of burnt ends, sausage, slaw, fried jalapeños and chipotle mayonnaise. It was an absolute explosion of flavors. While Char Bar honors the tradition of Kansas City pitmasters before them, they are taking the reins of advancing barbecue as we know it.

BRISKET BURNT ENDS

Burnt ends are flavorful pieces of meat cut from the "point" half of a smoked brisket. When brisket muscles are separated, the lean first cut (or flat cut) is the deep pectoral, while the fattier point—also known as the second cut, fat end or triangular cut—is the superficial pectoral. A traditional part of Kansas City barbecue, burnt ends are considered a delicacy in barbecue cooking, and no one does them better than Mitch.

COOK TIME: 15 hours   **YIELD:** 12 servings

1 (15-lb [6.8-kg]) whole brisket

4 cups (480 g) Meat Mitch Steer Season Rub, divided

1 cup (240 ml) Meat Mitch WHOMP! Naked BBQ Sauce

Trim the whole brisket to remove any excess fat, leaving ⅛ inch (3 mm) to caramelize during the cooking process. In a 12 x 20–inch (30 x 50–cm) pan that is 2 inches (5 cm) deep, season the brisket with 3 cups (360 g) of the Meat Mitch Steer Season Rub, making sure to coat it evenly and in every crevice.

Prepare the smoker to cook indirectly at 195°F (91°C) with a 12 x 20–inch (30 x 50–cm) water pan.

Once the brisket reaches an internal temperature of 170°F (77°C), about 8 to 9 hours, increase the smoker's temperature to a finishing temperature of 225°F (107°C). Cook for 1 hour.

After 1 hour, the brisket's internal temperature should be 180°F (82°C). Separate the brisket cap from the brisket flat. Season the flat with the remaining 1 cup (120 g) of Meat Mitch Steer Season Rub where the cap was separated. Wrap the flat in aluminum foil. Place the wrapped brisket flat back in the smoker and cook for 1 hour, until the brisket flat reaches an internal temperature of 188°F (87°C). Let the flat rest for 1 hour, then slice it for sandwiches.

Increase the temperature of the smoker to 245°F (118°C). Put the brisket cap into the smoker and cook for 3 to 4 hours. The burnt end (brisket cap) is finished once it reaches an internal temperature of 202°F (94°C) and is tender to the touch (it should be soft at the point and feel like gelatin).

Let the burnt end cool for 45 minutes. Cut the burnt end in half with the grain to avoid shredding the meat. Then cut it into 1-inch (2.5-cm) thick strips. Turn the strips on their sides and trim any excess fat and bark that is too tough. Cut the strips into 1-inch (2.5-cm) cubes against the grain. Serve with the Meat Mitch WHOMP! Naked BBQ Sauce.

SMOKED JACKFRUIT SANDWICH

This smoked jackfruit sandwich is a perfect example of the transformation of barbecue. It is not only flavorful and savory but also vegetarian.

COOK TIME: 1 hour   **YIELD**: 4 servings

SMOKED JACKFRUIT

2 lb (900 g) canned jackfruit in water, drained

Salt, to taste

Freshly ground black pepper, to taste

SANDWICHES

¼ cup (60 ml) Meat Mitch Char Bar Table Sauce

2 oz (60 g) sliced provolone cheese

4 egg buns, toasted

¼ large avocado, thinly sliced

1 oz (30 g) sliced jalapeños

Prepare the smoker to cook indirectly at 150°F (66°C).

To make the jackfruit, lay a large piece of plastic wrap on a work surface. Place the jackfruit on the plastic wrap in a single layer. Cover the jackfruit with the plastic wrap. Using a meat mallet, smash the jackfruit lightly (this will help break up large chunks and increase the surface area). Lightly season the jackfruit with the salt and pepper. Spread the jackfruit out over a cooling rack. Place the cooling rack in the smoker. Smoke the jackfruit for 1 hour.

In a medium skillet over medium heat, combine the jackfruit and Meat Mitch Char Bar Table Sauce. Place the provolone cheese on top of the hot jackfruit and let it melt. Place the jackfruit and cheese on the bottom of an egg bun. Top the jackfruit and cheese with avocado and jalapeño slices. Repeat the process to build the remaining sandwiches.

1070 Virginia Center Pkwy.
Glen Allen, VA 23059
www.coolsmokebarbeque.com

There might not be a more popular or iconic pitmaster than Tuffy Stone. Known as the Professor, Tuffy's methodical precision and obsession with barbecue make him one of the most influential people in the industry. He is a classically trained chef and began his culinary career while working under Alain Vincey in 1987 at Vincey's restaurant La Maisonette in Richmond, Virginia. A few years later, the former marine left the restaurant to start his own catering company alongside his wife, Leslie.

Tuffy has earned grand champion titles in nearly every major barbecue competition, including back-to-back wins at the American Royal World Series of Barbecue. He was named grand champion at the 2015 Kingsford Invitational, and he made a history-making run at the Jack Daniels World Championship Invitational Barbecue: In 2016, Tuffy and his Cool Smoke team made history at the Jack, becoming the only team to ever win the contest three times and the only team to take home back-to-back top prizes. In addition to his place atop the competition barbecue circuit, Tuffy has served as a judge for Destination America's *BBQ Pitmasters* for five seasons, traveled the world (including cooking for the troops in Kuwait and teaching classes at Meatstock in Australia and New Zealand) and cooked twice at the prestigious James Beard House in New York City. In 2018, Tuffy released his highly anticipated first cookbook, *Cool Smoke: The Art of Great Barbecue.*

POTATO SALAD WITH SOFT-BOILED EGGS

If you are going to host a summer barbecue, there is a good chance there is going to be a potato salad on the table. Tuffy has developed a recipe for a salad that is as savory as anything you will take off your grill. A salad with bacon, scallions and soft-boiled eggs is a must-try. You will not be disappointed and neither will your guests.

COOK TIME: 40 minutes   **YIELD**: 8 to 12 servings

MUSTARD DRESSING

½ cup (120 ml) apple cider vinegar

¼ cup (63 g) whole-grain mustard

1 tbsp (15 ml) honey

1 cup (240 ml) olive oil

Kosher salt, to taste

Freshly ground black pepper, to taste

POTATO SALAD

3 lb (1.4 kg) baby potatoes, assorted colors, washed

¼ cup (72 g) kosher salt, plus more to taste

5 medium eggs

1 large yellow onion, halved

3 bunches scallions

2 tbsp (30 ml) canola oil

Freshly ground black pepper, to taste

12 slices crispy cooked bacon, finely chopped

1 cup (143 g) drained bread and butter pickles

¼ cup (10 g) finely chopped fresh flat leaf parsley

⅛ cup (10 g) finely chopped fresh dill

2 cups (300 g) finely diced celery

To make the mustard dressing, whisk together the vinegar, mustard, honey, oil, salt and pepper in a medium bowl and let the dressing sit at room temperature.

To make the potato salad, place the potatoes and salt in a 4-quart (3.8-L) pot over high heat. Cover the potatoes with cold water and cook at a slow boil until they are just tender, 8 to 10 minutes. Drain the potatoes and let them cool to room temperature.

Place the eggs in a small pot, cover them with cold water and bring them to a boil over medium heat. Once the water boils, remove the pot from the heat. Cover the pot and let the eggs sit for 6 minutes. Drain the eggs and place them in a bowl of ice water until they are cool.

Prepare the grill to cook directly at 300°F (149°C).

Cut the potatoes in half lengthwise. Lightly coat the potatoes, onion halves and scallions with the canola oil, salt and pepper and place them on the grill. Grill the potatoes, cut-side down, for 10 minutes. Begin flipping the potatoes occasionally and cook for 10 more minutes, until they are crispy and tender. Grill the onion halves for 6 minutes, flipping occasionally. Grill the scallions for no more than 1 minute on each side, making sure not to burn them. Set the onion halves and scallions aside to cool. Once they have cooled, thinly slice them.

In a large bowl, combine the grilled vegetables with the bacon, pickles, parsley, dill and celery. Toss the mixture gently with 1 cup (240 ml) of the mustard dressing and adjust the seasonings to taste.

Transfer the potato salad to a serving platter. Peel and halve the eggs and arrange them on the platter. Drizzle the salad and eggs with some additional mustard dressing and serve at room temperature.

ACKNOWLEDGMENTS

Make sure to pick the right teammate. Your relationship needs to be a team mentality, one that shares a common goal, ambition and drive. Most people grossly underestimate what it takes to start a business. I'm thankful to have someone who not only understands what I'm trying to do but supports and motivates me. Everyone wants to be the sun that lights up your life during the good times. But not her—she wants to be my moon, providing me with the light to help me shine during my darkest hour. Noelle, the past few years have absolutely flown by. I feel so blessed, fortunate and thankful to be able to fall in love with you each day. You can run with the devil in a world that knows only how to walk. Life isn't about waiting for the storm to pass. It's about learning how to dance in the rain.

If someone comes up to me at an event and asks me what my role in the company is, I often say, "I'm the truck driver and dishwasher who just happens to also sign the checks."

You can't do it alone. No matter what your current role in your career, there will come a time when you need the help of others to reach peak levels. When I initially tell a member of the team my job is to train them to take my job, they look at me with confusion. My job as a leader is to unlock their potential, to empower them to be decision makers. I trust them with our brand as if it were their own, and to be frank, it is as much theirs as mine. If I can train them to take my job, then I can focus on new opportunities and ventures for us.

Being able to work alongside our crew is a privilege. John Witherel, you are more than my right hand—you are a great man and a great friend. Thank you, Katie "Kay Slay" Thoman, for having the passion to want to learn. From working the pits to changing the beer taps, you have never shied away from learning and being a leader. Heartfelt gratitude to our Handsome Devil Family: Andy, Annilee, Erica, Eloise, Jillian, Alyse, Dayna, Allie, Hurricane Nancy, B-boostin, Cody, Josh, Bella, Donnie, the Rios girls, Casey and numerous other BOH/FOH team members who have donned the spade over the years to help us shine on a daily basis.

Sincere thanks to those who have helped support our brand. Storm Sasaki, without you, my friend, who knows if we would be here today. You gave a start-up company a chance.

Greg Nivens, Trigger Agency and Drink.Eat.Relax family: Thank you for the incredible opportunities you give us. Your events are often imitated but never duplicated. Even though whenever we do a show in the South, you make it a point to let the crowd know we are from New York, we still love ya.

Paul Lloyd, Anthony Verano, Ben English and Mike Fusco, thank you for seeing the value we bring to an event and continuously working with us to make great events for the Hudson Valley even better.

Rick DiLeo, your constant support and business acumen is something I always will appreciate. You allow me to focus on the task at hand while helping position us for the future. Cool, cool, my friend.

Thank you to Jerry Higbie and the entire HigFab company, a championship race team and fabrication business that selflessly promotes our brand. Jerry, you are always there for us, whether rebranding your team to better promote us or fabricating a new banner system for our concession trailers. You are just another example of local small businesses supporting one another. We are proud to be a part of the HigFab family.

I wish every author could be so lucky to work with a photographer as talented as Ken Goodman. Ken, you are a true professional; to be able to work with you and see how you capture the soul of each photo is priceless.

Thanks to Will Kiester and Marissa Giambelluca at Page Street Publishing for being open to this concept that is different, daring and fun. You allowed me to pursue my passion while giving me the tools to succeed. This has been an adventure I will never forget, and I hope it is just the beginning of our working relationship.

To every pitmaster I met on the road, thank you. My grandfather once told me, "There is a time in your life you might not have much, but one thing no one can take from you is your pride." I hope you are as proud to be a part of this book as I am. We shared our passion, had some great laughs and helped raise money for Operation BBQ Relief.

Everything I own today I owe to my parents, Ed and Joan Randolph. They taught me the value of money, the difference between right and wrong and the importance of hard work. They allowed me to make decisions while letting me learn there were consequences for those decisions.

Everything you see and read about in this book is the result of motivation I receive from my girls, Lily, Emma and Amai. Girls, you will never know how your smiles make me want to move mountains. I hope every parent has a child who likes to cook, learn, laugh and love with them. I'm lucky to have three. To the moon, my loves. I hope to always make you proud.

ABOUT THE AUTHOR

Ed Randolph is the founder, owner and pitmaster of Handsome Devil BBQ. Randolph and Handsome Devil BBQ received national attention when they won the 2017 Food Network New York City Wine and Food Festival for best barbecue, followed up with 2018 awards for Best BBQ in the Hudson Valley, New York, and at the NJ BBQ Showcase at Westfield Garden State Plaza. Randolph, who grew up in the farming-rich area of Hudson Valley, New York, absorbed cooking techniques from his Italian mother and Polish grandmother.

Randolph's ambitious, all-hustle approach has taken the Handsome Devil brand from the rural backwoods to the bright lights of the city. Appearing at more than fifty events a season, the Handsome Devil team has traveled from Windsor, Vermont, to South Beach, Miami Beach, Florida, to compete and share their barbecue with the public. In 2014, the Handsome Devil team was recognized by the barbecue community for their efforts and invited to be the barbecue vendor for the Memphis in May World Championship Barbecue Cooking Contest in Tennessee—the first time someone from New York had been asked. In addition to the Food Network championship, the Handsome Devil team has amassed state championship awards in six states and has catered events for numerous Fortune 500 companies, movie premieres for Warner Bros. and other high-profile events, including the New York Air Show, the Taste of Country Music Festival and the Beer, Bourbon and BBQ Festival.

As a small-business owner, Randolph understands the importance of community. He is a contributor to Operation BBQ Relief, local veterans organizations, youth organizations and Beyond Type 1. He also pursues his passion for auto racing with his Higbie Family Race Team. Randolph currently resides in Newburgh, New York with his wife, Noelle, and daughters Lily, Emma and Amai.

INDEX